MARISSA KESTER

Guidebook to the Apocalypse

History, Myth, and the Cycles of Civilization

PYTHIA
PRESS

Until you make the unconscious conscious, it will direct your life and you will call it fate.
— C.G. Jung

Contents

Introduction

Everywhere you look, something is coming undone. Conflict, institutional breakdown, and rapid cultural fragmentation seem to meet us at every turn. The future no longer appears as a horizon beckoning us forward, but as an ominous fog.

If you've felt unsteady or quietly afraid, you're not alone. This isn't just personal anxiety. It's the signature of an age shifting. In mythic terms: we are in the underworld.

Not as punishment, but as initiation.

Across cultures, descent into the underworld has always marked the moment when the old version falls away and transformation truly begins. This is that moment we find ourselves in right now. The world many of us were raised to believe in has ended, a new one is forming, and we are in the liminal space between the two. Things feel messy, unpredictable, and unnerving, to say the least. How do we navigate a moment such as this?

That's where Guidebook to the Apocalypse comes in.

Like many of you, I've spent the past few years trying to make sense of a world that feels like it is unraveling and reorganizing at the same time. What began as a historian's curiosity slowly turned into a map. I followed a trail across disciplines like astrology, history, economics, climate data, myth, and systems theory…and something unexpected began to reveal itself. I realized all of these separate fields were describing essentially the same cyclical patterns, just using different language. What looked like chaos at first began to show rhythm. And when you can see rhythm, you can orient.

That is what this book offers. Not certainty, but orientation. In times of upheaval, people do not need another prediction. They need a way to place themselves inside the moment. To locate their position within a larger pattern so they can respond with clarity rather than panic.

Orientation is what allows a sailor to navigate a storm. Not because they control the sea, but because they can read the sky. They know when to adjust the sails, when to seek harbor, and when to ride the current. Cyclical literacy functions the same way. It does not promise control over the future. It offers context for right action in the present.

This book is a framework for orientation. A way of seeing the moment we are in, not as random collapse, but as a patterned transition within a longer arc of time.

Before we start, I want to be clear about what this book is *not*. It is not purely astrological. It is not strictly geopolitical. It is not just a history text. It is not academic, nor is it a casual essay or blog post. It sits in the space between disciplines where pattern recognition tends to hang out.

It took me five years to pull all of this together in what I hope is a somewhat coherent format. If left unchecked, I could spend fifty more weaving in additional cycles, data sets, and references. I've left out far more than I've included because this is not meant to an encyclopedia. It is a guided overview. A doorway to a new way of thinking and perceiving our current state of affairs. For everything that didn't make it onto these pages, I'll continue expanding through future editions and my digital work.

This book is also not fear-mongering. It is not "buy my course to survive the apocalypse." I'm not a prophet, a prepper, or someone claiming to know exactly what's coming. Everything in here—the war cycles, economic rhythms, astrological timelines—comes from researchers, economists, historians, astrologers, and thinkers who did most of the heavy lifting long before I came along. My contribution is synthesis, or noticing the pattern behind the patterns and offering it in a way that can be used.

The era we are living through is a transition, not a collapse into nothingness. Think of late winter: gray, stagnant, seemingly lifeless. If you had never lived through a full cycle of the seasons before, you might assume it would stay that way forever. That's what our nervous systems do under the prolonged stress of our civilizational winter—they assume the current state is permanent. But bigger seasons are turning right now and spring always comes.

Believing that isn't delusion. It's pattern literacy.

But that doesn't mean we get to sit back and "trust the process" while eating popcorn. Spring requires physical preparation, just like birth. And yes, I use that metaphor very intentionally. We are in the transition phase of labor right now. Anyone who has gone through birth or witnessed it closely knows this is not the soft, candlelit montage version you see in movies. It's intense, disorienting, and it requires a different mindset than ordinary life. You prepare not to control the outcome, but to stay present through process. You gather resources, support, resilience, and you accept that something must die so something new can be born.

In this case, what is dying is our industries, narratives, currencies, mythologies, and versions of ourselves we thought we would be. Versions of the world we thought were permanent. We don't get spring without the death of winter, and we don't get a new world without the intensity of birth.

This book exists to help you recognize the process for what it is. My hope is that by the time you finish these pages, you feel less frantic and more grounded. Less focused on immediate outrage and more oriented toward the broader arc unfolding beneath it all. If one cycle in this book sparks something in you—good. Follow it. Go deeper (and welcome to the dark side).

Most of all, I hope this book helps you remember that we are not outside the process, watching history happen. We are inside it, shaping it with the way we choose to see.

Together We Rise,

Marissa Kester
    October 24, 2025

1

The World is Ending. But Not Like That.

There is a time for everything,
and a season for every activity under the heavens:
a time to be born and a time to die,
a time to plant and a time to uproot,
a time to kill and a time to heal,
a time to tear down and a time to build,
a time to weep and a time to laugh,
a time to mourn and a time to dance,
a time to scatter stones and a time to gather them,
a time to embrace and a time to refrain from embracing,
a time to search and a time to give up,
a time to keep and a time to throw away,
a time to tear and a time to mend,
a time to be silent and a time to speak,
a time to love and a time to hate,
a time for war and a time for peace.

Ecclesiastes 3:1-8 (NIV)

Let's start with something you already know. Something you already feel.

The world is ending.

You can *feel* it. Sense it. In your bones. In your communities. In the spaces between headlines and deep sighs. In the eyes of your friends or coworkers as you discuss current events, politics, or the state of the world. The systems that you grew up with that once seemed so solid and larger than life now seem hollow. The truths you grew up believing now feel naïve and childish. The promise of a better future doesn't land the way it used to. What once looked like destiny now just looks like theater. The illusion is gone.

You're not crazy.
  You're not broken.
  You're awake.
  And this book is for you.

You, my dear reader, are one of the few trying to make sense of the unraveling happening all around us. You want to understand what is happening and not just get swept up in the drama of it. You probably recognize all the old stories are falling apart. Not just out there in the world, but maybe inside you too.

You might not have the language for it yet, but you know this moment isn't just about politics or climate or capitalism or social division. It feels bigger. Older. Mythic. Maybe even a bit familiar. Like we've reached the end of something so vast, we don't even have a name for it.

And that's because we have.

But the world isn't ending in the Hollywood sense (sorry to spoil the fun). It won't end with a bang, or a meteor, or zombies (and if it does and I'm wrong this book will also disappear with it. How's that for plausible deniability).

It's ending in the way that worlds always do: slowly, unevenly, and from the inside out.

What we're experiencing isn't just the collapse of institutions or the failure of systems. It's the death of a paradigm. A worldview. A collective myth. One that has shaped the modern world for centuries and is now breaking down under the weight of its own contradictions.

Right on time.

The exciting part is that we've seen this before. In fact, we've lived through it before. The Bronze Age collapse. The fall of Rome. The end of feudalism. The Industrial Revolution. Each time, it felt like the end of the world. And in some ways, it was. But it was also the beginning of something else. Something that right now is still brand new, unfamiliar, and not yet fully formed.

This book is not a roadmap out of collapse or a manual for preppers or a manifesto for the end times. Quite the opposite. It's a guide to the deeper story, or what I call sacred cycles. The mythic, astrological, psychological, and energetic layers that help us make sense of where we are, and what might be emerging through the rubble.

Because beneath all the noise and breakdown, there's something else happening: an unveiling. A remembering. A return.

We are not here just to survive the apocalypse. We are here to lean in and midwife what comes next.

Let's begin.

* * *

Before we dive into the juicy, mythic terrain of this book, I want to take you back in time. Because one of the most helpful ways to make sense of our moment is by comparison. And few moments energetically echo ours quite like the Bronze Age Collapse, circa 1155 BCE.

If you've never heard of it, here's the gist: about 3,180 years ago, a whole interconnected world unraveled.

The great civilizations ringing the ancient Mediterranean—Mycenaean Greece, Egypt, the Hittites, Minoans, Canaanites—all bound by trade, treaties, shared tech, and elite alliances somewhat suddenly fell apart. Like us, these people had international diplomacy, shipping networks, and economies built on complex webs of cooperation. It was, for its time, a globalized world.

And then, in the span of a century, it all fell apart.

Cities vanished. Writing systems disappeared. Palaces crumbled. Famine spread. Refugees fled. Sea Peoples (still a mystery) arrived. People tried to explain what had happened, but most didn't know. All they probably knew, in that moment, was that the world they knew, that felt permanent, wasn't.

Historians still argue over the cause. Climate instability? Earthquakes? Invasion? Corruption? Complexity? The answer is probably yes, pieces of all of it. A cascade of interwoven crises that pushed everything past a breaking point. What historians call a *system collapse.* And when it all collapsed, it ushered in centuries of chaos and contraction followed slowly by the birth of something new.

Sound familiar?

We similarly live in a hyperconnected world. Global systems nested within global systems. Supply chains. Energy grids. Algorithms. Institutions no one trusts but everyone relies on. And now, like then, we're watching the cracks spread: ecological strain, geopolitical tension, social fragmentation, spiritual exhaustion…collapse seems to threaten from around every corner.

But collapse doesn't have to mean the end of everything. What it does mark though is the end of one thing: the way we see the world and our place within it. And with that ending comes the messy, mysterious beginning of something new.

And this is where we are right now.

We are not living through the end of **the** world. We are living through the end of *a* world. Which happens to be our world.

Ours may be built on silicon instead of bronze, but the parallels are striking: elite overreach, environmental degradation, brittle supply chains, cultural disillusionment. And most tellingly, a pervasive sense that something is off. That the stories we've inherited no longer make sense.

I'm a professional historian and former intelligence analyst with over 15 years of experience and multiple degrees. But let me be clear: I'm not a geopolitical forecaster, an oracle, a guru, an economist, or your mom telling you what to believe or do. Brilliant minds are already mapping this unraveling through the lenses of politics, economics, energy systems, and demographics. They parse election outcomes, model supply chain vulnerabilities, debate climate tipping points, and analyze shifting power centers from Washington to Beijing. Some focus on technological acceleration (AI breakthroughs, automation, the rise of digital currencies) while others examine cultural trends like social media's impact on collective consciousness and the generational divides reshaping society's mood. These perspectives are crucial, and I've taken as many as I can into consideration while researching and writing this book, but the overall theme of this work takes a different path.

My gift lies in seeing patterns, particularly the invisible threads that weave these patterns together. That's what we'll explore here: the unseen architecture of our current apocalypse. The mythic, astrological, and psychological terrain beneath the headlines. This is the realm of Pluto's underworld transit, the Saeculum's winter, and the turning of the Great Year. Sound woo woo? I promise these aren't just poetic metaphors. They're archetypal cycles. Deep rhythms that show up in different guises and using to different language across cultures, traditions, and industries. To historians they are world systems, generations, or Saecula, to astrologers as outer planet transits, to economists as Kondratiev Waves. Each language a doorway into the same paradigm shift. And they are all deeply, painfully accurate and applicable right now.

The Threshold

If history tells us anything, it's that civilizations don't simply explode or vanish overnight. They slowly erode. Spiritually, structurally, symbolically. Collapse creeps in when the web of meaning can no longer hold. When the stories that held everything together stop making sense and people stop resonating with the storytellers.

That's the tension you feel now: the bone-deep fatigue, the sense of two worlds colliding. It's not just you. It's not just anxiety. It's not the other political party, the toxins in the environment, or the boomers. It's the psychic weather of paradigm shift. This is what it feels like to stand at the threshold— caught between what was and what will be, with little insight into, or control over, either.

In mythical language, this is the *liminal space*. The threshold space. The realm of the goddess. The shadowed corridor between unconscious and conscious, ether and matter. Here we meet Hecate at the crossroads, Persephone in descent and return, Inanna stripped bare in the underworld, Isis piecing back what was broken. The underworld is also a gateway to the void: a place of dissolution and incubation, where the old self, system, or paradigm dissolves so the unimagined can be born. In this territory, we cannot map or control. We move only by the torchlight of our own intuition.

In other words, we are driving through a snowstorm and can only see as far as our headlights in front of us (which if you've ever done this, is not far).

Because we're not simply watching institutions fail. We're feeling the tectonic plates of reality itself shift beneath us. The myth of endless progress is unraveling. The binaries that shaped the modern age—mind and body, spirit and matter, self and other—are being exposed.

It is disorienting. But it can also be liberating.

Because collapse isn't just destruction. It's *revelation*. It's the peeling back of illusions.

The Modern World at a Turning Point

The Bronze Age collapse gives us one powerful mirror, but there's another closer to home: the fall of Rome.

In 476 AD, a messenger arrived in Italy carrying a letter that quietly ended an empire. The boy-emperor Romulus Augustulus was ordered to step down. Just like that, Rome—the empire that had defined the known world for centuries—was gone.

But, as with the Bronze Age, Rome didn't vanish overnight. That letter was only the final punctuation mark. The unraveling had been in motion for decades, even centuries. Corruption hollowed out the empire's core. Plagues swept through its cities. Borders buckled under relentless pressure.

Trade routes collapsed. And Rome's once-mighty legions were increasingly outsourced to mercenaries with little loyalty to the empire they served. The story of Rome as eternal, divine, and destined to rule no longer held.

For the people living through it, it must have felt like the end of the world. Institutions disintegrated, literacy declined, and economies slowed to a crawl. Later historians would call what followed the "Dark Ages."

But just as with the Bronze Age, it wasn't darkness everywhere. In the East, Byzantium carried on Rome's legacy for another thousand years. From the 8th century onward, the Islamic Golden Age became a flourishing center of science, medicine, and philosophy, preserving and expanding ancient knowledge before eventually sending it back to Europe. Across the globe, in Tang Dynasty China, in India, in Mesoamerica, great civilizations thrived while Europe struggled. The light of culture and learning had not gone out; it had simply shifted and taken root elsewhere.

Looking back, we can see Rome's fall not just as failure but as metamorphosis. One skin shedding so another could grow. Monasteries safeguarded sacred texts. Local kingdoms carved out fresh identities. The seeds planted in this so-called "darkness" would eventually sprout into the Renaissance and the modern nation-state. What looked like collapse was, in truth, a winter. And winters are always followed by spring.

Apocalypses are rarely instant or universal. They are slow, uneven, and local. For one region, collapse feels like the end of the world. For another, it may look like renewal, opportunity, or even flourishing. The same pattern echoed in the Bronze Age collapse, and again in Rome's decline. What looks like death in one place is often gestation in another.

And here we are again. It's easy to look around and see only unraveling as systems fail, polarization deepens, and trust in institutions or the future dissolves. To panic, stockpile beans, or build bunkers. But winter is not the end. It is part of the cycle. Old systems are meant to decay and die. Sometimes suddenly, but more often slowly and in ways we've been watching for years. The hardest part is allowing it. Because without winter, there can be no spring. No possibility of renewal.

This is the task we are faced with now. Not just the practical work of navigating the very real consequences of change, but the deeper task of surrendering old stories, moving through disorientation, and finding the courage to step into the unknown.

For me, the best way to do that is the focus on about spring. That means tending the soil, trusting the process, and getting crystal clear on the metaphorical seeds we want to plant—the ideas, values, and visions we want to see take root and thrive in the new paradigm. This moment, standing at the end of old cycles and the threshold of new ones, demands both short-term resilience and long-term imagination.

And I know what you might be thinking: *Marissa, this sounds inspiring, sure— but isn't it a little too rose-colored? I want to believe transformation is possible, I really do. But part of me feels like this is just spiritual spin, a way to "feel good" while everything is burning down around us. Aren't we just on a steady march toward annihilation?*

And in the imaginary conversation I'm having with you right now, here's what I'd say back: *I completely understand why you might think that. But that conclusion is based on the faulty premise that collapse can only ever mean the end. That belief is the backbone of the very paradigm, the very story, that's now unraveling.*

And it's that story—the myth of endless progress, of control, of linear destiny—that we're here to question.

The Myth of Progress: The Heroic March Forward

The modern Western world tells itself a grand story. It begins in darkness, with humanity weak and primitive, barely scraping by. But then, armed with reason and determination, we rise.

We imagine ourselves emerging victorious. Sword in one hand, iPhone in the other. Bloody yet triumphant from our long heroic journey out of ignorance and superstition into the rational light of modernity. The world, once chaotic, has been subdued. Nature has been conquered, knowledge has been mastered, and civilization has reached its peak.

This is the Myth of Progress. The belief that history is a linear ascent, and each step forward is an improvement upon the last. It is the foundational story embedded in Western consciousness, reinforced through education, religion, and our institutions. And like all myths, it can be deeply comforting. Yes, suffering has been necessary. Yes, sacrifices have been made. But the end justifies the means. Everything, from war and colonization to environmental destruction, has been for "the greater good."

At the heart of this story stands the hero, personified as a masculine force and stoic conqueror, who rises above nature and tradition to slay the dragon of ignorance. He bends the world to his will through sheer might and intellect. His crowning achievements are science, technology, and global dominance.

The Myth of Progress is so deeply embedded in Western thought that it rarely gets questioned. It doesn't present itself as a paradigm, but as *reality itself*. Simply "the way things are." This myth is foundational to everything, including our sciences and theories about how the world works. Which, as you can imagine, is a problem because when science (or any other discipline) grows from a faulty assumption, it ends up reinforcing that same assumption. We've built a miniature world inside a much larger one and then mistaken it for the whole.

This myth reassures us that despite setbacks, we are advancing. That technology, governance, and rational thought will eventually solve all problems. That we are living at the pinnacle of human evolution.

Yet for all its seductive promises, the Myth of Progress is in silent competition with another story that is equally powerful and equally pervasive. One that offers a starkly different vision of where we've come from and where we're headed. Instead of a heroic march forward, it paints a picture of decline and something precious lost along the way.

The Myth of the Fall: The Lost Golden Age

The second great myth tells a very different story. It, too, envisions a long journey of progress, but in the opposite direction.

In this telling, humanity was once whole. We lived in reciprocity with nature. Our daily lives dictated by the rhythms of land and sky, intimately connected to one another and to the cosmos. Life may have been simple, but it was saturated with meaning. The sacred was not something "out there" but instead pulsed through the everyday.

Then, something changed.

With the rise of agriculture came permanence, surplus, and hierarchy. Fields required boundaries, and boundaries required protection. Land could now be owned, hoarded, or taken. Surplus food gave rise to inequality, wealth, ruling classes, and dental cavities. What began as a survival strategy soon seeded a new mindset—one centered on scarcity, security, and control. Instead of seeing themselves as part of nature's cycles, humans began to see themselves as managers of it.

What was once sacred became profane, segmented, and systematized. The pursuit of progress and power came at an unbearable cost: disconnection. Modern history, through this lens, is not a story of steady advancement but of falling away from wisdom, from harmony, from the sense of belonging to a living cosmos. The rise of agriculture, cities, empire, capitalism: each layer brought new complexity, longer lifespans, but also more separation. Somewhere along the way, we lost our connection to the divine. And with it, we lost ourselves.

From this perspective, modern civilization is not a triumph but a tragedy. Industrialization, materialism, technological dominance…the very forces that define our world today are seen as symptoms of a deep spiritual wound. Rather than ascending toward enlightenment, humanity has been moving further and further from its true nature.

The consequences of this fall are everywhere. The environmental destruction we now face is not an accident. It is a direct result of our disconnection from the Earth. The mental health crisis and widespread existential despair are not random, but symptoms of a civilization that has lost its soul. The modern world, despite all its advances, feels increasingly hollow, as if something vital has been lost.

This story is woven into ancient myths and modern fears alike. It is the tale of Atlantis, the lost civilization that thrived in wisdom and technology until its own corruption destroyed it. It is the story of Eden, a paradise where humanity once lived in divine unity, only to be cast out into a world of suffering. And it's echoed today in the rising nostalgia for a (hypothetically) simpler, off-grid lifestyle—the collective longing to return to a lost paradise.

The False Choice

Both the Myth of Progress and the Myth of the Fall offer compelling narratives. One celebrates an upward march toward enlightenment, the other laments a tragic descent into corruption. Both have profoundly shaped modern thought, but neither tells the whole story.

The Myth of the Fall feels undeniable. Something has been lost. The modern world can feel hollow, disconnected, and artificial. The pursuit of growth has severed humanity from deeper rhythms and truths. Where nature was once seen as sacred, it is now something to extract and control. Technology pulls many further from embodied experience, while industry and empire drive cycles of war, exploitation, and environmental destruction.

And yet, this story romanticizes the past, overlooking the brutal realities of earlier life—disease, famine, high infant mortality, and hierarchies of their own. The image of a peaceful, egalitarian paradise is as misleading as the notion that history has been an uninterrupted climb toward progress. (People have always peopled. Our ancestors were no more perfect than we are.)

Humans have a well-documented tendency toward nostalgia. This is what psychologists call "declinism bias," or the belief that the past was better than the present and that the future will only get worse. We yearn for what we imagine we've lost: a simpler childhood, a golden age of history, a time when life felt more connected and meaningful.

On the other side, blind faith in progress carries its own distortions. Modern culture runs on the assumption that history moves in a straight line, each stage more advanced, enlightened, and evolved than the last. The same breakthroughs that save lives also created nuclear weapons, industrial warfare, and mass surveillance. Industrialization lifted many from poverty while devastating ecosystems that we depend on for survival. The digital age connects us, yet fragments our attention, frays our relationships, and breeds new forms of distress. For every advancement, there is an unintended and generally unforeseen consequence. This fantasy of inevitable improvement is as simplistic as the nostalgia for a lost mythical golden age.

Both myths feel true.

The result is a deep ambivalence at the core of modern life: part of us convinced everything is unraveling, another part compelled to keep building anyway. We are stretched between despair and hope, nostalgia and vision.

Constantly torn by the weight of two stories pulling us in opposite directions. Both the Myth of Progress and the Myth of the Fall tug at us, but they share the same foundation: the belief that time moves in only one direction.

But time is not a straight line. It bends, loops, and repeats.

Seen through that lens, we realize that both myths contain truth, but only in their respective season. What looks like ascent or decline is simply one curve of a larger, repeating pattern. The background rhythm by which civilizations rise, fracture, and renew.

This is the third story, the one our ancestors knew but we've mostly forgotten: time moves in cycles.

Cycles: The Ancient Map for a New Reality

We know the seasons turn, the moon waxes and wanes, tides rise and fall, bodies are born and die. Women's hormones cycle every 28 days, men's every 24 hours. Animals migrate and have babies at the same times each year. Cycles are everywhere, dictating the natural world all around us. And yet, when it comes to the human story, for some reason we believe we've escaped them. As if we're the first ones clever enough to outsmart the wheel.

The idea of time as a straight line is actually a recent invention, not a universal truth. For most of human history, people didn't see the world this way. They saw what nature reveals: time as a spiral, a wheel, a rhythm. From the Yugas of ancient India to the Mayan Long Count to the Greek Great Year, civilizations across the globe mapped time not as an arrow but as a return. This didn't mean they had all the answers, or that they were able to circumvent the inevitable winters (just look at the ruins of ancient cities that scatter the planet), but they carried a perspective we've largely lost, and urgently need to recover.

Re-incorporating the idea of cyclical time back into our zeitgeist requires us to get really comfy with impermanence. Or how the cliché goes: the only thing constant in life is change. Empires rise, stagnate, fall. Ideas bloom, wither, revive. Paradigms expand until they can no longer hold and then something new begins. None entirely better or worse than the other. Just different. And all necessary.

We struggle because, well that is the human condition, but also because our modern Western culture has forgotten this. We built our world on the illusion of endless forward motion. On productivity charts, GDP curves, startup scaling plans, and 10-year visions for global domination. We believed our tools and optimism would save us. That we could outbuild, outthink, and out-hack entropy.

But entropy always has the last word.

What makes this moment so disorienting isn't just the chaos around us. It's the mismatch between reality and the story we've been telling about it. Linear time doesn't explain what to do when "forward" stops working. It never prepared us for limits, collapse, or paradigm shifts. We've been taught to trace causes and effects along a straight line, when in truth they're only symptoms of a deeper cycle. A natural turning of the wheel.

This moment is the transition between seasons. Like when pumpkin spice lattes are on the menu, but you are still wearing shorts and a tank top. We are living through a weaving of opposites, where birth and death, loss and renewal, are entwined.

This liminal space, inherently full of paradox, isn't failure. It's design.

The Romans believed their empire was the pinnacle of civilization. So did the British. So did the Ottomans, the Mongols, the Spanish crown. So does Silicon Valley. Every age tells itself the same story of permanence and destiny.

But the universe whispers the same quiet truth: *you are not the exception.*

Yes, we live in extraordinary times. But no, they are not entirely unprece-dented. The shape is familiar. The details are new, but the energy is old. Once again, our paradigms, those invisible operating systems we barely notice that dominate for centuries, are being shattered and replaced. And the beliefs we treat as self-evident truth? One day they'll look quaint. Outdated. Maybe even absurd.

We are not outside the cycle. We are inside it. We always have been. And that's the medicine of this moment: not panic, but perspective. We've been here before. We'll be here again. The world isn't ending, it's turning.

Cycles Are Reality's Operating System

Once we begin to see time as a spiral rather than a line, an entire dimension of reality comes into view. We realize that change is not random, but rhythmic. That life does not simply progress, but has a rhythm. That beneath the surface of chaos, there is a structure, a pattern, and timing to life.

Cycles are the invisible architecture of the world. They govern the body, the Earth, and the cosmos. They are the repeating rhythms through which life renews itself: expansion and contraction, birth and death, ascent and decline.

We live within layers of cycles every moment of every day. Some are immediate and easy to feel: the inhale and exhale of the breath, the circadian rhythm that regulates sleep and wakefulness, the hormonal cycles that shape mood, energy, and appetite. Others are more subtle: the seasons of the year, the phases of the moon, the slow unfolding of physical and psychological development. And then there are larger cycles still. Those that shape not just individual lives but generations, nations, ecosystems, and civilizations.

None of the cycles operate alone. They are nested. Smaller cycles within larger ones, who are within larger ones still. All of them interlocking like gears in a great cosmic machine. When one turns, it affects the others. Fast cycles (like breath) move frequently. Medium cycles (like economic patterns or generational shifts) turn more slowly. Larger cycles (like civilizational epochs or planetary alignments) may unfold over centuries or millennia.

Yet they all move. And when multiple cycles turn at once (especially those at the medium and large scales) we experience what feels like a moment of collapse or breakthrough. The ground shifts. History speeds up. What once felt stable becomes fluid.

This is where we are now.

Astrology as a Language of Cyclical Time

To navigate change on the scale we are living through, data alone is not enough. Information tells us what is happening, but it rarely tells us where we are within the arc of a larger story. For that, we need an ability to perceive pattern, timing, and symbolic meaning to give us orientation. This is where astrology comes in. Most skepticism toward astrology isn't rooted in evidence but in unfamiliarity with how it functions and the kind of value it offers. It is not superstition or simple prediction, but a framework for reading time.

Astrology is one of humanity's oldest pattern-recognition systems. Long before spreadsheets and economic models, people tracked shifts in culture, harvests, weather, the collective mood, and even the trajectory of empires by observing movements in the sky. Not because the planets were believed to cause events, but because they appeared to resonate with them, marking distinct energetic qualities in time. In modern language, we could say astrology works more like a quantum field indicator than a mechanical force. The planets do not push or command, they provide "windows of opportunity." For example, when Pluto is in the sign and in this place, we usually see violent revolutionary activity.

The planet's positions in the sky relative to one another reveals another layer, helping us understand where we are within a cycle and what specific archetypal dynamics are active. Understand what these patterns mean (astrology) is like reading a tide chart before going boating rather than thinking you can just get out there and then control the ocean.

Cycles form the backbone of every discipline that studies life or civilization. Historians from Plato and Ibn Khaldun to Spengler and Toynbee mapped the rise and decline of cultures as recurring arcs. Economists track business and credit cycles. Biologists study circadian and hormonal rhythms. The language changes, but the underlying truth remains: life moves in patterned waves. Astrology simply offers a symbolic lexicon for those waves, refined over millennia.

At its core, astrology is the study of time and archetype. Each planetary cycle marks a different tempo of unfolding. Fast cycles like the Moon's speak to emotional tides and collective sentiment, while long cycles like Pluto's trace the lifespan of nations, ideologies, and structural power. Again, these planetary bodies do not dictate outcomes. Rather, they act as cosmic timekeepers, signaling when certain archetypal forces like innovation, decay, rebellion, war, etc. tend to surface within the collective. We can use tools like an ephemeris to see where the planets will be and get a sense of the "windows of opportunity" ahead, but astrology is far closer to pattern recognition and archetypal psychology than fortune-telling.

The modern world has trained us to see time as a straight line—an endless march of progress or collapse. Astrology restores a different memory: that time spirals, that history echoes, that energy condenses and releases in rhythm. It reintroduces a mythic awareness and language into our analysis of world events, not to escape reality but to contextualize it within an active, living pattern.

And this really matters, especially now. We are moving through a period where our linear systems—economic, political, psychological—are breaking down under their own weight. In moments like this, orientation becomes a survival skill. Astrology offers an in-depth orientation. Not by telling us what will happen, but by revealing what kind of time we are in now and what is around the corner. Knowing the season doesn't eliminate uncertainty, but it makes uncertainty navigable.

Astrology offers a compass, not a script. It is an ancient language that has evolved over time to match the myths of the culture using it. It has long helped humans recognize where the energetic current is flowing so we can move with it rather than against it. It helps us remember that we are participants in a patterned universe, not random actors in a meaningless one.

For the rest of this book, we will examine the five major cycles currently turning over right now. Each contributing individually, as well as altogether, to the immense transformation underway. The interwoven cycles outlined in this book are maps of timing and archetypal pressure. Together, they explain why this moment feels so profound. Because it is.

With that compass in hand, we can now turn to the five major cycles shaping our era.

The Five Big Cycles

1. The Social Cycle (20–30 years)

These are the cycles we feel most intimately in culture because they are about people. Every generation carries a specific psychological imprint shaped by its upbringing, historical context, and inherited memory, and contributes to the constant shapeshifting of social norms.

Social cycles explain why values evolve, why certain narratives rise and fall, and why each generation seems to react to or rebel against the one before. In the West, this cycle length closely mirrors the "generational turnover" described in Strauss and Howe's saeculum theory, as well as astrological transits like Pluto's movement through the zodiac, Saturn's return, and the lunar nodal axis. When social cycles reach their peak, we experience widespread questioning of identity, belonging, and belief alongside an increased tension between groups.

2. The Resource Cycle (50–60 years)

These cycles track the rise and collapse of economic and technological paradigms. They govern how we generate energy, wage war, move capital, and extract value from the world. Each turn initiates a wave of innovation—followed by dislocation.

Economists call these Kondratiev Waves: long surges of growth fueled by new technology, always followed by breakdown and restructuring. Joseph Schumpeter named this pattern creative destruction, or basically old systems die so new industries can emerge. Each cycle introduces a new resource logic: coal and rail, oil and steel, digital and data, now AI and automation.

But every resource breakthrough carries a cost. Social fabric tears. Labor value shifts. Environmental strain increases. When this cycle turns, the world doesn't just adopt new tools but also rewrites its economic story. We are standing in that rewrite now.

3. The Institutional Cycle (80–100 years)

Institutional cycles trace the lifespan of the systems we build to maintain order: governments, education, medicine, finance, media. These structures are born to solve a certain problems, they mature into stability, and eventually decay—not necessarily from corruption (that is a side effect), but from their inability to solve today's problems.

Roughly every century, the operating logic of a society breaks. The American Revolution, the Civil War, World War II were all institutional resets triggered when existing systems could no longer hold the complexity of their era. Today, we are in another late-phase cycle: institutions built after 1945 are losing legitimacy. The institutional system of the old world is failing and something new is organizing beneath it.

4. The Global Cycle (~500 years)

Global cycles track the rise and fall of world-systems. Not just governments or economies, but the entire container that defines how civilization organizes power, identity, and meaning. As you'll see in the Global Cycle chapter, institutions don't exist in a vacuum. They sit inside a larger civilizational framework, and when that framework hits its limits, no institution survives unchanged.

For the past five centuries, the dominant world-system has been the European led marriage of capitalism and the nation-state, born from the ashes of feudalism and fueled by industrial expansion. It behaved like all world-systems do: it delivered order and growth for a time, then began to exhaust itself. Today we are witnessing the late phase of that cycle — where legitimacy erodes, currencies strain, empires tighten their grip even as their reach diminishes, and the center of gravity begins to shift away from the powers that once felt permanent. What looks like geopolitical chaos from the ground is, in long-wave perspective, the turning of a five-hundred-year wheel.

5. The Epochal Cycle (2,000+ years)

Epochal cycles operate on mythic time. They do not simply reorganize politics or economics but rewrite the spiritual operating system of humanity.. As you'll see later in the manuscript, ancient cultures from India to Egypt to

Greece tracked these turns through the Great Year, the Yuga Cycle, the Long Count, and the Precession of the Equinoxes. Each epoch carries a symbolic frequency. The Piscean age, organized around illusion, sacrifice, belief, and spiritual abstraction, is dissolving. In its place, an Aquarian frequency is emerging—decentralized, pattern-based, collective, technological, and integrative. Transitions on this scale are not clean or comfortable. They are liminal, initiatory, and disorienting by design. We are not just living through a historical moment, but the end of a world age and the birth of another.

Taken together, these cycles reveal that we are not living through random chaos but a layered initiation.

Civilization is not ending. The next paradigm is being revealed.

Apocalypse: An Unveiling

I choose the title *Guidebook to the Apocalypse* not because I think we're hurtling toward some Hollywood-style doomsday, but because I believe we're living through an apocalypse in the truest sense of the word.

Did you know that the word *apocalypse* doesn't actually mean "the end of the world?" That popular idea gained traction in the 19th century, when evangelical preachers reframed the Book of Revelation as a countdown to imminent global destruction. In truth, the word comes from the Greek verb *apokalyptein* which means to uncover or to reveal. An apocalypse is not, at its core, annihilation. It is *unveiling,* or a moment when illusions fall away and hidden truths come into view.

That's what this moment is. And that's why this book exists: to serve as a guide through the unveiling. Because if all we see is chaos, we miss the invitation to participate in the turning of the wheel with eyes open.

Of course, unveiling doesn't necessarily mean gentle. Apocalypses come with their share of darkness and discomfort. No one enjoys having their illusions, institutions, or expectations stripped away. It's disorienting, to say the least. As I've been hinting, collapse is an essential part of the process. And while some of it can be fiery and sudden, most of it unfolds as a slow erosion of meaning and the realization that the stories we've relied on to point us toward success, identity, safety, and the future no longer make sense.

It's also uneven. One person may be in the fire of transformation while their neighbor scrolls TikTok and orders takeout. That's not a contradiction; it's how apocalypses unfold. In waves, in layers, uneven across time and geography. Less like a bomb, more like a tide. And tides, as we know, always return.

If it makes you feel better, every civilization has had its turn in the barrel: Rome, feudal Europe, the Ottomans, the Mayans, the Khmers, Songhai, Egypt, Greece. The agrarian world before industry. The industrial economy before artificial intelligence and quantum computing. Each assumed it would last forever, until it didn't. And what came after was never a neat improvement, but a remix.

Seen this way, apocalypse is less an ending than an initiation. The Stoics called it *ekpyrosis*—the fire that destroys one world to make space for the next. In Hindu cosmology, it is Kali's dance of destruction and renewal. In astrology, it is Pluto's descent into the underworld. There is always a breaking apart before a becoming.

Which brings us to now.

The Threshold

What's collapsing isn't just our institutions. It's the lens we've used to make sense of them. The belief that we stand apart from cycles, nature, and history, somehow exempt from the patterns that shape every living thing, is coming undone.

And beneath it? Something older. Something truer.

This isn't just an economic crisis, a technology shift, or a political rough patch. It's not your neighbor's fault, or that political party, or any particular race, gender, or identity. It's not something we can pin on one group, one leader, or one ideology. What we're experiencing is bigger than any single scapegoat. It's a fundamental turning in the human story. A collective reckoning with the stories we've all inherited and the systems we've all participated in. Blame may feel comforting, but it won't move us forward. This moment asks us to step beyond finger-pointing and start seeing the deeper patterns at play. Patterns that invite each of us to take responsibility for the world we're creating.

The end of the Bronze Age wasn't just a geopolitical unraveling; it was a collapse of the old world's organizing principles and systems. Both then and today represent the end of an age of global interconnection under stress, with cascading crises challenging old powers and opening the space for new civilizational models.

The difference is that today we're aware of these cycles, and we have tools (science, global communication, technology) that could potentially either cushion collapse or accelerate it.

If the cycles could talk to us they would say: see the energy for what it is and use it wisely. Don't try to predict the future or fix everything overnight. But really learn to see clearly. To question the lens you've inherited, explore the deeper patterns shaping your world and recognize the myth you've been living inside so you can begin aligning yourself with a different one.

Because the end of an old paradigm isn't the end of the story. It's the turning of the wheel in the great spiral. A chance to remember deeper wisdom, and to carry it forward, transformed.

Physicist Carlo Rovelli, in his exploration of time, argues that what we call "time" is not a fixed feature of the universe but a perceptual artifact of change. According to his interpretation of quantum theory, the flow of time exists only because we cannot perceive every detail of the universe all at once. Time emerges from relationship, or the differences between one moment and the next. He writes:

"The world is not a collection of things, it is a collection of events. The hardest stone is, in reality, a complex vibration of quantum fields... a process that for a moment holds a shape in equilibrium before disintegrating again into dust."

In other words, reality is not composed of objects, but of transformations. Change is inescapable. And time is how we make sense of change.

A cyclical view of time tells us that nothing is wasted. That death feeds life. That seasons return. That timing matters more than force. That beginnings and endings are not opposites, but partners. It invites us into attunement rather than control. To live inside this paradigm is not to regress. It is to return to a way of seeing that is both ancient and urgently relevant.

In the next chapter, we will explore the first of these five great cycles: the Social Cycle. Here is where we come to understand how generational patterns, psychological inheritance, and collective memory shape the cultural mood of an era.

Because before we can understand the world, we have to understand the *people* in it.

2

The Social Cycle

Cycle Length	• 20-30 years (Pluto/Generation) • 80-120 years (Saeculum)
Featured Cycles	• Pluto ingress into new sign • Generational Theory • Saeculum & Fourth Turning framework
Next Cycle (approx.)	Late 2020s-2110s • New generation in 2023 • New saeculum late 2020s
Key Themes of Social Cycle	• Collective mood shifts • New founding mythology/villain story for next cycle • Mirrors Institutional Cycle (ch. 5)

Every generation feels like it's living through the most pivotal moment in history. And in a sense, it is. The headlines shift, the technology evolves, and the culture wars change costumes, but beneath it all, the same rhythm plays out: people building, breaking, and balancing the world they inherit. This is the Social Cycle, and it is the heartbeat of human history. It's not driven by policy or innovation alone, but by collective psychology: what we believe, what we fear, and what we choose to create or destroy together.

Every generation plays a character or role in this story of society. Some are builders. They lay foundations, construct new systems, and dream up better worlds. Others are dismantlers. They are born to question, to deconstruct, to burn down what's clearly not working. And then there are the stabilizers, the ones who hold the middle ground, tending the balance between the two. Together, these three archetypal roles form a living trinity of forces: Creation, Destruction, and Neutrality.

This trinity isn't moral; it's ecological. It's what keeps societies alive. Creation without destruction breeds stagnation; destruction without creation leaves only ruin. Neutrality, though quieter, is what maintains coherence through the chaos. Every era, every movement, and every generation participates in this dance.

The Social Cycle reminds us that history isn't just a linear timeline of events; it's a reflection of *us*. Our conversations, our conflicts, our inventions, our ideals, our solutions to problems (and the problems themselves) are all expressions of the same timeless rhythm. The easiest way to see this trinity in motion is through people themselves. Each generation carries one of these roles—builders, breakers, or balancers—playing out the next act in the story of society's evolution.

What Is a Generation?

Boomers ruined the housing market. Millennials killed napkins. Gen Z is too online.

At first glance, generational talk sounds more like clickbait than cultural insight. Marketers use it to sell us things, politicians use it to divide or inspire us, and social media thrives on the endless back-and-forth of who had it harder, who had it better, and who ruined what. Every week brings new headlines, jokes, or blame games pitting one age group against another. It's an ongoing soap opera we all seem to instinctually understand and find our place in. Why is that?

Because beneath the memes and marketing gimmicks lies something deeper. The concept of generations is one of the longest-running, universally recognized rhythms of social change. From the genealogies of the Old Testament to the myths of the Greeks, Hindus, and Celts, humans have long used the rhythm of generations to make sense of time itself. Each lineage, each "house," was a way to map both ancestry and destiny. Individually and strung together, generations help tell the story about how the past becomes the present, and the present becomes the future.

At its simplest, a generation is a group of people born within a shared window of about twenty to thirty years. What makes them more than demographics, though, is their *shared biography*, or the imprint of formative events, conditions, technologies, and cultural moods they are born into. This cohort moves through life together, experiencing the same major events and conditions through youth, adulthood, and old age. A child, a teenager, and a parent who all experienced 9/11 lived through the same event but carry entirely different stories of it. That's the secret of generations: they don't just live through history; they *interpret* it, each through their own lens of time and stage of life. Generations are the lenses through which we view history, and in turn, how history views us.

Over time, these cohorts take on distinct personas, or characters in the great novel of human society. They're born, they grow, they rise, and they fade, each convinced they've cracked the code of life until the next generation rewrites the rules.

Modern society tends to imagine history as a straight line of progress (always forward, always up). But the commonly understood concept of generations reveals something else: a cycle. The moods, values, and archetypes of one era eventually return, reshaped but familiar. It's not that one generation is better or worse; each simply occupies a different season in the larger rhythm of time. And seasons, like taxes, come around again and again.

For centuries, humans have understood this idea through the metaphor of the seasons: childhood as spring, youth as summer, maturity as autumn, old age as winter. The same rhythm applies not only to individuals but to cultures and civilizations. Native American teachings speak of the Four Hills of Life; Hindu philosophy describes the four ashramas, or stages of spiritual and social growth; the Greeks divided life into four ages. Across traditions, the wisdom is the same: life unfolds in seasons, and those seasons repeat.

In other words, generations move through these seasons together, carrying shared experiences, challenges, and callings.

So, while pop culture reduces generations to stereotypes (entitled Boomers, fragile Millennials, doomer Gen Z) the truth is that each carries a unique psychic weather system: a collective memory and nervous system shaped by its season of history. That's why generational tension feels so personal. It's not just ideological; it's experiential and somatic. Seen this way, no one generation is dysfunctional or a mystery. They're all operating the way they are by design. They're how humanity self-corrects over time. One wave rebels, another refines, the next rebuilds. Each inherits the imprint of the age before it, and each prepares the ground for what comes next. Together, they create the rhythm of history.

* * *

So how do we decide who goes in what category? Where does one generation end and another begin?

The common practice today is to delineate generations in retrospect. This is typically done by generational researchers and is based on a variety of factors, such as demographics, attitudes, historical events, popular culture, and prevailing consensus among researchers. It is not an exact science, and different researchers will likely have different takes on why and when one generation ends and another begins.

As you might imagine, with this method the lines of demarcation between generations can be…fuzzy. This is to be expected. As much as our brains (and current worldview or paradigm) might try to convince us otherwise, humans and humanity rarely fits neatly into a box or number line. The energy of change is not compartmentalized or sealed off. The universe doesn't seem to care to match the way we choose to measure and track time.

But, lucky for us, there is much more helpful way to draw the line between generations. One that not only gives a more accurate understanding of the persona of each generation, but also provides a higher purpose to the zeitgeist of each age.

That tool is Pluto.

Pluto: The Cosmic Clock

Built into the very rhythm of our solar system is a universal, energetic demarcation of generations: Pluto.

Discovered in 1930 and originally dubbed *Planet X*, Pluto takes its name from the Roman god of the underworld who is the keeper of wealth, death, and rebirth. To understand Pluto's energy, think of nuclear fission (discovered the same decade): a force both creative and destructive, splitting atoms to unleash unimaginable power. Within months of Pluto's discovery, the world was plunged into the Great Depression. The decade that followed saw the rise of organized crime, fascism, and global war. These manifestations are all representative of our collective descent into the underworld of power, fear, and survival.

Archetypally, that's how Pluto works. It dissolves what has decayed in order to regenerate what must emerge. It exposes the hidden, transforms shadow into substance, and reminds us that destruction is part of creation's process.

* * *

The Archetype of Pluto

Across the world's mythologies, the same "Pluto" energy reappears under different names and forms. This archetype is the keeper of thresholds, the guardian of hidden power, and the one who destroys in order to renew. Whether portrayed as god or goddess, this figure presides over the invisible realms where endings become beginnings.

In Greece and Rome, Pluto and Hades ruled the underworld not as monsters, but as necessary custodians of balance who guarded the wealth buried beneath the earth. Beside him stood Persephone, whose descent and return each year ensured the world's renewal. In Egypt, Osiris was torn apart and reborn as lord of the afterlife, while Anubis guided souls across the threshold with a steady hand. Mesopotamian myth tells of Ereshkigal, queen of the great below, whose dark domain offered transformation to those brave enough to descend just as her sister Inanna did, dying to her former self and rising changed.

Far to the east, the Hindu god Yama and goddess Kali embody the same force: death as justice, destruction as liberation. Kali dances upon illusion, devouring ego so that truth may live. Up north, Hel sits upon her shadowed throne, half-beautiful and half-decayed, reminding mortals that wholeness requires both. The Celtic Cailleach and Morrigan wield winter's scythe and war's chaos to strip away what has grown stale, clearing the field for new life.

Even in the Americas, this pattern repeats. The Aztec Mictlantecuhtli and his consort Mictecacihuatl reign over the land of the dead, guardians of bones and renewal. In Japan, Izanami transforms from creator to death goddess, showing that every birth story contains its shadow. And in mystical Christianity, the energy lives on in figures like Mary Magdalene, the initiator of death and resurrection mysteries, and in the alchemical stage of nigredo, where all things must first decay to reveal their gold.

Every culture has its version of Pluto to remind us that descent is initiation, not punishment. The archetype teaches that what we fear as ending is only transformation in disguise. In the underworld's silence, life rearranges itself for the next beginning.

* * *

Astrologically, the sign Pluto is moving through describes the collective energy Earth is experiencing at that time, and the imprint it leaves on those born under its influence. Because Pluto moves so slowly, everyone born within a given 12–30 year span shares Pluto in the same sign. Each of these groups, or generations, carries a distinct evolutionary theme: the aspect of society that their generation is destined to transform.

For example, between November 5, 1983, and November 10, 1995, Pluto was transiting Scorpio. Anyone born during those years, if they looked at their birth chart, would find Pluto in Scorpio (though its *exact position* in their chart depends on their birth time and place). For this generation, Pluto in Scorpio colors how the cohort experiences power, transformation, and the confrontation with shadow at the societal level. It marks a period when collective energy is drawn toward exposing hidden truths, purging what's decayed, and reclaiming what's been suppressed.

In this way, Pluto's sign reveals where deep psychological and structural change is unfolding in the collective. Everyone has Pluto somewhere in their birth chart, and the sign it occupies describes the shared lessons, fears, and transformations of that age group, or the soul work of an entire generation.

Pluto takes roughly 248 years to complete one orbit around the Sun, spending 12 to 30 years in each zodiac sign. Because of this slow pace, everyone born under the same Pluto sign shares an energetic imprint, or generational identity, shaped by transformation at a particular layer of civilization.

Pluto Through the Signs (Tropical Zodiac)

Approximate Date Ranges by Transit

Pluto Sign	Years (approx.)	Themes this generation will have to deal with/ Generational Arc
Aquarius	2023 – 2043	Reformation of systems, AI, decentralization, collective reinvention
Capricorn	2008 – 2023	Collapse and restructuring of institutions, authority, and power hierarchies
Sagittarius	1995 – 2008	Globalization, ideology, information expansion, belief wars
Scorpio	1983 – 1995	Taboo confrontation, shadow integration, sexual and psychological transformation
Libra	1971 – 1983	Relationships, justice, equality, the collapse of traditional partnerships
Virgo	1957 – 1971	Work, health, efficiency, the rise of systems thinking and environmental awareness
Leo	1939 – 1957	Ego, leadership, creativity, nuclear power, and the cult of individuality
Cancer	1913 – 1939	Home, nationalism, emotional security, upheaval of family and homeland
Gemini	1882 – 1913	Communication, technology, early globalization, education reform
Taurus	1851 – 1882	Industrialization, material wealth, land, ownership, and economic consolidation
Aries	1822 – 1851	Revolution, individualism, emergence of modern nation-states
Pisces	1798 – 1822	Mysticism, religion, empire dissolution, end of old orders
Aquarius	1778 – 1798	Enlightenment, revolution, human rights, social experimentation

For example, those born when Pluto was in Cancer (1912/1913–1939) were shaped by themes of family, security, and sacrifice. They came of age during the Depression and World War II and went on to build the suburban, domesticated world of the 1950s. The Baby Boomers, with Pluto in Leo were born with a fiery sense of self-expression and destiny, fueling the cultural revolutions of the 1960s and 70s. Later Pluto placements in Scorpio, Sagittarius, Capricorn, and now Aquarius describe Millennials, Gen Z, and Gen Alpha, each with their own archetypal imprint and built in generational quest.

Of course, we all have to deal with the same overarching themes as Pluto moves through each sign. For instance, right now we are all encountering the themes of Pluto being in Aquarius. But the way we deal with those issues (decentralization, AI, etc.) will be colored by the Pluto sign we were born under and have experienced life through. That is our permanent, generational lens.

Pluto's movement through the zodiac is like a slow drumbeat beneath the surface of history. It does not describe individual personalities but generational archetypes. Where Strauss and Howe identified Prophets, Nomads, Heroes, and Artists, Pluto layers on archetypes of depth: the family protectors of Cancer, the self-expressive rebels of Leo, the critics and reformers of Virgo, the justice-seekers of Libra, the shadow-divers of Scorpio, the philosophers of Sagittarius, the institution-challengers of Capricorn, and now the innovators and revolutionaries of Aquarius.

In November 2024, Pluto fully entered Aquarius, beginning a new generation. The last time Pluto was in Aquarius was during the American and French Revolutions, eras defined by the radical reimagining of governance, power, and collective identity. We are also deep in a Fourth Turning Crisis. Together, this energy brings themes of decentralization, technological transformation, collective sovereignty, and a total rewrite of how we organize society.

* * *

The Pluto Generations at a Glance

Pluto's slow march through the zodiac creates generational cohorts, each tasked with transforming a particular domain of life. The bullets below outline these Pluto generations through the last century, showing how the archetypes of each sign expressed themselves on the world stage.

**Pluto's orbit is eccentric, meaning that some generations are double the length of others. Additionally, when Pluto transitions to another sign it will go in and out of that new sign for a year or so before it fully transitions to the new sign. This is why you might see some weird date overlap. This is what Pluto was doing in 2023 when it made a brief visit to Aquarius.*

Pluto in Cancer (1912–1939) — GI / Silent Generation

- Keywords: Sacrifice, security, family, nationhood
- Key Events: WWI, Great Depression, women's suffrage, rise of fascism, Roaring '20s
- Core Themes: Home and family redefined through displacement and economic hardship; nationalism surges as empires collapse and fascism rises; transformation of security through crisis and adaptation; a patriotic, survival-focused generation that laid the groundwork for the postwar world.

Pluto in Leo (1937–1958) — Baby Boomers

- Keywords: Self-expression, leadership, drama, identity
- Key Events: WWII, nuclear age, Cold War, decolonization, suburbia, rise of celebrity culture
- Core Themes: Power and leadership through global dominance and charismatic figures; individual expression erupts through youth rebellion and celebrity mythology; destruction and rebuilding in the nuclear age and postwar reconstruction; a era defined by cultural revolution,

prosperity, and personal identity.

Pluto in Virgo (1956–1972) — Late Boomers / Early Gen X

- Keywords: Service, duty, analysis, improvement, equality
- Key Events: Civil Rights movement, sexual revolution, counterculture, space race, computing revolution, environmentalism
- Core Themes: Work, health, and service become sites of reform; efficiency and innovation through automation and the space age; rising skepticism and analytical scrutiny of authority; a transitional archetype moving from self-glorification to collective humility and systemic correction.

Pluto in Libra (1971–1984) — Gen X / Xennials

- Keywords: Relationships, fairness, justice, balance
- Key Events: Feminism, divorce revolution, Roe v. Wade, OPEC/G7 formation, Cold War détente
- Core Themes: Relationships and partnerships restructured through divorce, co-parenting, and renegotiation of gender roles; justice and equality movements expand civil and LGBTQ+ rights; diplomacy and globalization create interdependence and mediation-based leadership; aesthetics and media shape culture, producing a generation of mediators and cultural interpreters.

Pluto in Scorpio (1983–1995) — Older Millennials

- Keywords: Depth, power, taboo, transformation
- Key Events: End of Cold War, Gulf War, AIDS crisis, grunge era, globalization, Human Genome Project
- Core Themes: Power and control renegotiated through geopolitical shifts and corporate dominance; taboo and mortality rise to public awareness through AIDS and shadow themes; regeneration expressed

through environmentalism and digital underground culture; secrets and corruption exposed, marking a generation of alchemists dismantling what no longer serves.

Pluto in Sagittarius (1995–2008) — Younger Millennials / Gen Z

- Keywords: Philosophy, exploration, belief, freedom
- Key Events: 9/11, War on Terror, EU expansion, internet and social media rise, refugee crises, Harry Potter and Lord of the Rings mythic revival
- Core Themes: Belief systems transform through religious shifts, ideological clashes, and pluralism; global awareness expands through travel, trade, and internet connectivity; knowledge accelerates in the information age, reshaping education and worldview; truth and ethics become battlegrounds amid misinformation and polarization.

Pluto in Capricorn (2008–2024) — Gen Z / Gen Alpha

- Keywords: Structure, order, maturity, sustainability
- Key Events: Global financial crisis, COVID-19, populism, AI rise, climate crisis, #MeToo
- Core Themes: Transformation of authority through institutional collapse and accountability movements; systemic breakdown triggers the dismantling of hierarchies; sustainability and survival become core values amid climate and economic instability; technology and surveillance infrastructures dominate and redefine power structures.

Pluto in Aquarius (2023–2043) — Gen Alpha (Emerging)

- Keywords: Innovation, revolution, networks, collective power
- Key Events: AI revolution, decentralization, technological leaps, global reorganization echoing American and French Revolutions
- Core Themes: Innovation and rebellion overturn outdated systems,

redistributing power to networks and communities; collective identity forms through digital tribes and decentralized belonging; law, technology, and social contracts are reimagined in favor of inclusivity and autonomy; a revolutionary generation tasked with redefining what it means to be human in a post-system world.

* * *

Remember the concept of a generation moving through seasons? Well, as Pluto moves 30 degrees from its birth position, it "aspects" itself, marking pivotal moments in our lives and in the collective life of a generation. Each aspect carries its own energy: some are transformative and intense, others gentler and more reflective. Over a lifetime, we may experience up to six of these aspects, each signaling a shift not only for ourselves, but for our generation as it transitions into the next phase of life.

You can feel these shifts not just personally, but culturally. Each sign of the zodiac irritates the one before it, so different generations (i.e. different Pluto signs) naturally do not jive with one another. Adjacent signs have different elements and modalities (fire clashes with water, earth with air, etc.) creating friction that *fuels* generational change. It's no wonder we often struggle to understand the generation following us; their energy feels foreign, unsettling, and entirely new.

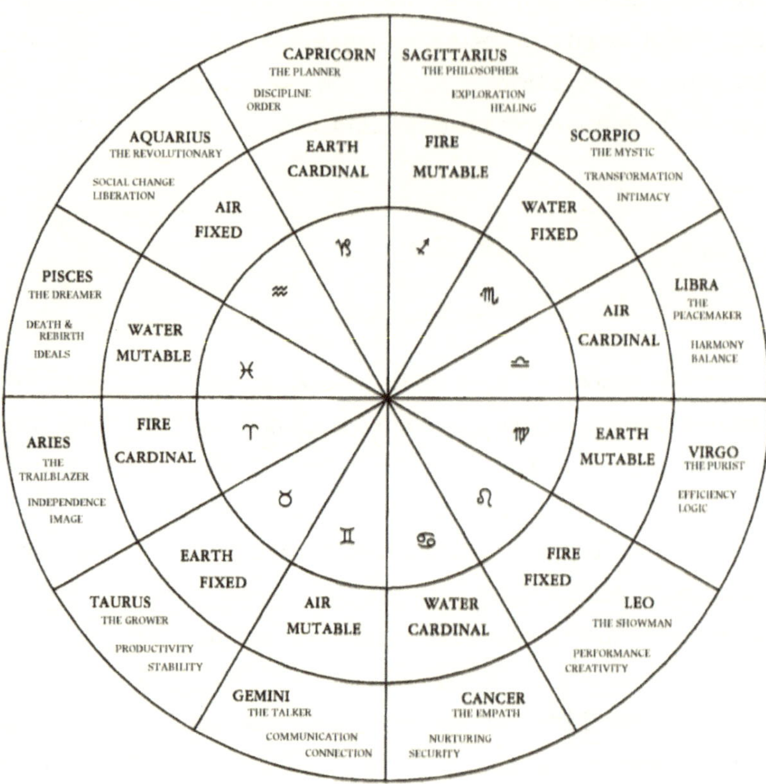

In recent decades, Pluto's faster orbit has compressed these generational shifts. Generations are smaller, their lifespans shorter, and their impact more intense. This acceleration is why life (and time) today feels like it's moving at breakneck speed. It's also why we feel catapulted toward transformation or chaos depending on our perspective. It's not that social change is new, it's that Pluto is moving faster, cramming more change into a single lifetime than many previous generations have known (at least since the late 17th century).

But as with all celestial rhythms, there's a story being told here. Pluto's passage through each sign of the zodiac represents a chapter in a collective tale, one that cannot be skipped or rushed. Each generation inherits the torch from the one before it, carrying the lessons, struggles, and triumphs forward. To understand where we're going, it's always helpful to look back at the last century of Pluto placements. Each sign tells a part of the story that has shaped us, and will shape what comes next.

* * *

Case Study: Pluto in Capricorn & Aquarius

Pluto in Capricorn (2008–2023)

Capricorn rules over hierarchy, government, corporations, and institutions. It also rules the Father (or Patriarch) and is ruled by Saturn, the planet of time and structure. Pluto's passage through Capricorn forced a global reckoning with power and the structure, or bones, of civilization. Over these fifteen years, the structure clearly began to show signs of stress.

- **2008 Global Financial Crisis:** The era began with collapse. The same systems that defined "stability" imploded under their own weight. Faith in economic and political leadership fractured, and populism surged to fill the void.
- **Authoritarianism and Populism:** From Brexit to Trump to a global rise in nationalist movements, collective trust in elites eroded. Citizens rebelled against bureaucracies they felt no longer served them.
- **Collapse of Trust:** Religion, government, media, and corporate power all faced crises of legitimacy. Corruption and inequality became impossible to ignore.
- **Technology and Surveillance:** Big Tech consolidated power while reshaping economies, politics, and even identity. The internet became both a tool of liberation and a mechanism of control.
- **Social Movements:** Occupy Wall Street, Black Lives Matter, #MeToo, and climate activism exposed systemic injustice and demanded account-

ability.
- **COVID-19 Pandemic (2020–2021):** The global crisis revealed institutional fragility and deep inequities, shattering the illusion of "normal."

Themes: Pluto in Capricorn stripped away illusion. It exposed the hidden rot beneath the marble halls, dragging abuses of power into the light. Governments, corporations, churches, and hierarchies were tested to breaking point. The archetype of the *Patriarch*—authority, structure, and control—met its reckoning. What could not bend broke. What could not adapt dissolved.

The work of Capricorn was to lay bare the failures of the old world, preparing the ground for what comes next. And what comes next is Aquarius: the archetype of innovation, collective power, and radical reimagining.

Pluto in Aquarius (2023-2044)

If Capricorn was about control, Aquarius is about circulation. Aquarius demands "power to the people," decentralization, and the power of the network. The question is shifting from *Who's in charge?* to *How are we connected?*

The Last Pluto in Aquarius (1778–1798)

The last time Pluto moved through Aquarius, the world reinvented itself. Revolutions—political, scientific, industrial, and spiritual—shattered the foundations of the old order. Monarchy and divine right gave way to democracy and secular governance. Power left the palace and entered the public square.

- **The American Revolution:** Born under Pluto in Capricorn, it matured under Pluto in Aquarius. The U.S. Constitution (1787–1789) enshrined ideals of representation and equality—radical concepts for their time.
- **The French Revolution:** Beginning in 1789, France overthrew monarchy and aristocracy in a fervor of idealism and terror. The people

demanded "liberty, equality, fraternity"—and paid for it in blood.

- **The Haitian Revolution (1791–1804):** Enslaved Africans rose up, winning independence from France and founding the first Black republic. It was a global earthquake that terrified empires and proved that freedom could not be owned.
- **Science and Innovation:** The late 18th century marked the birth of the modern world. Electricity was identified and harnessed. The metric system emerged as a rational ordering of reality. The steam engine, astronomy, medicine, and chemistry all accelerated.
- **Ideas and Ideals:** Thinkers like Mary Wollstonecraft, Thomas Paine, and Immanuel Kant expanded notions of rights, equality, and reason. Human identity shifted from fate and bloodline to participation in the social contract.

Themes: Hierarchies collapsed. Collective ideals surged. Technology leapt forward. Consciousness itself changed. Humanity redefined what it meant to be free.

Pluto in Capricorn tore down the old hierarchies. Pluto in Aquarius is here to build what will become the foundation for next 100 years (at least). The last time this transit occurred, empires fell and nations were born. This time, it may be systems of data, governance, and belief that dissolve and reconstitute. As Pluto enters Aquarius, power disperses from institutions to networks, from hierarchy to community, from centralization to decentralization. The emphasis moves from authority to autonomy, from tradition to experimentation.

* * *

The generation born under Pluto in Aquarius (today's babies) won't just inherit this world. They'll be native to it. Much of their lives and frameworks will emerge in dialogue with machines. Their myths will be shaped not by national borders but by the global web of influence they're born into. They won't ask, "How do I fit into this system?" They'll ask, "Why does this system exist at all?"

While they carry the seeds of the future, us adults (particularly the Pluto in Libra/Scorpio/Sagittarius generations who are their parents) carry the burden of being the bridge. Pluto in Capricorn children were tasked with dismantling outdated systems. Pluto in Aquarius children will reimagine them.

The Saeculum

Alright we've walked through the concept of the generation. We understand the generations do not exist in isolation, but as part of the larger rhythm of the social cycle. We know that generations have lifespans, or in other words they are born, live, grown old and die. That concept is what the ancients called the saeculum.

* * *

The Roots of Generational Theory

While Strauss and Howe gave us the modern language of four turnings, the idea of recurring generations and saeculums is not new. Cultures across time and place have recognized that history unfolds in generational waves. What Strauss and Howe did was synthesize these threads into a clear framework of four archetypes and four "turnings" — a cycle of ~80–100 years that we can still trace in history today. Here are some other dudes with similar ideas:

* ***Polybius (c. 200–118 BCE):*** *Greek historian who described anacyclosis,*

the natural rotation of political systems from monarchy → aristocracy → democracy → tyranny → renewal. His model implied that each form, like a generation, carried the seeds of the next.

- ***Biblical & Mythic Genealogies:*** *From the Old Testament's "begats" to Greek heroic lineages, ancient peoples mapped time through family descent. Generations weren't just markers of biology; they were the architecture of sacred history passed down through time.*

- ***Ibn Khaldun (1332–1406):*** *In Muqaddimah, he described dynasties lasting three to four generations (~120 years), dynasties last roughly three to four generations (~120 years), evolving from vigor to decadence before collapse (an articulation of the saecular rhythm).*

- ***Chinese Dynastic Thought:*** *The Mandate of Heaven was said to endure about three to four generations before Heaven withdrew its favor. Renewal required moral and social restoration, mirroring the natural turnover of human lifespans.*

- ***Niccolò Machiavelli (1469–1527):*** *In* The Discourses on Livy, *he observed that republics and institutions decay over time and must be periodically renewed—often through crisis or reform—roughly every century.*

- ***Giambattista Vico (1668–1744):*** *In* The New Science, *he described history as moving through recurring "Ages of Gods, Heroes, and Men," a triadic cycle of cultural evolution and decline.*

- ***Auguste Comte (1798–1857):*** *His "Law of Three Stages" (theological → metaphysical → scientific) reflected humanity's cyclical intellectual maturation, a social evolution that would later influence sociological models of generational change.*

- ***José Ortega y Gasset (1883–1955):*** *Argued that each generation defines itself by reacting to the one before it, advancing history through tension and renewal* (The Revolt of the Masses).

- ***Karl Mannheim (1893–1947):*** *In* The Problem of Generations, *he reframed the concept sociologically: what binds a generation is not age alone but the formative events that create shared consciousness.*

- ***Carl Jung (1875–1961):*** *His work on archetypes and the collective unconscious suggested that generational cycles are psychological as much as* *historical—patterns replaying through the deep structures of the human psyche.*

- ***Etruscans and Romans (c. 7th–1st century BCE):** The word saeculum comes from Etruscan cosmology, later adopted by the Romans, and referred to the natural lifespan of a human generation or civilization, or the time from the birth of one person until the death of the last who witnessed that birth. The Etruscans believed each civilization was allotted a finite number of saecula (often ten), after which divine renewal (or destruction) would occur. The Romans turned it into a civic cycle, marking the end of each saeculum with the Ludi Saeculares, or "Secular Games," a ritual of purification and renewal held roughly every 100–110 years.*

* * *

The Latin word *saeculum* meant a "lifetime," or the natural span of a human life, roughly 80 to 120 years. This would equate to about four or five generations if we follow Pluto's rhythm as our guide. Just as an individual moves through childhood, youth, maturity, and old age, so too do societies and the institutions they create. Building on this ancient idea, historians William Strauss and Neil Howe proposed in *The Fourth Turning* (1997) that history doesn't advance in random fits and starts but in repeating cycles with each roughly the length of one long human life. Within each *saeculum*, time unfolds through four distinct seasons, or "turnings," each lasting about twenty years.

- **High (Spring):** Institutions are strong, individuals are weak. Society feels united, optimistic, and confident about the future.
- **Awakening (Summer):** Institutions are questioned. Spiritual renewal and cultural rebellion break out. Individuals grow stronger, pushing back against conformity.
- **Unraveling (Fall):** Institutions weaken, trust declines, culture frag-

ments. Cynicism rises. Individualism peaks.

- **Crisis (Winter):** The old order collapses or is reforged through upheaval. Collective survival becomes the priority.

Each generation is shaped by the turning it is born into and then goes on to play a particular archetypal role:

- **Prophets (Boomers):** Born after a Crisis, indulged as children, they grow up to lead Awakenings.
- **Nomads (Gen X):** Born during an Awakening, they grow up neglected and cynical, becoming pragmatic survivors in midlife.
- **Heroes (Millennials):** Born during an Unraveling, protected as children, they come of age in Crisis, tasked with rebuilding.
- **Artists (Gen Z):** Born during a Crisis, they are overprotected and sensitive, destined to become adaptive, creative adults.

Together, these archetypes move the cycle forward. Prophets stir the visions, Nomads test the systems, Heroes build them, and Artists refine them.

Each time Pluto enters a new sign, the next generational archetype is born. This is what Strauss and Howe might describe as a turning within the larger generational rhythm. Each ingress also represents a shift in collective power structures and cultural obsessions as a new archetype rises into adulthood and leadership.

The Next Social Cycle (Late 2020s-2110s)

We've covered a lot of ground in this chapter, but when you zoom out, I hope the rhythm of the social cycle comes into focus. Generations, marked by the sign Pluto is in, are the heartbeat of social change. Every time Pluto changes signs a new archetype emerges and the collective focus shifts. Every 4-5 of these archetypes form a story arc, or saeculum. This saeculum is the life story of those 4-5 archetypes and how they individually and altogether are born, live, and die.

Right now, we're in what Strauss and Howe call the Fourth Turning, or the winter of our current *saeculum*. Pluto's move into Aquarius in 2023 ended fifteen years of Capricorn's institutional reckoning and ushered in a twenty-year era of technological upheaval and social decentralization.

Today's social crises are not just random symptoms or the effects of *fill in the blank* cause. They're signals of transition. The saeculum gives us the framework. Pluto gives us deeper context. Generational tension, ideological polarization, and institutional change are the friction points through which evolution happens.

Each generation has its role to play in that turn. One holds the memory of what was, another dreams what could be, and somewhere between the two, the next world begins. This moment, as one social cycle ends an another begins, is the handoff. The torch passing between eras.

In the next two chapters we will expand from the social cycle into the closely intertwined socioeconomic and war cycles.

expand so rapidly that a money economy overtook the self-sufficient one. More on this in Chapter 6.

Think of it this way: resource cycles create the terrain. Social cycles determine how people react to that terrain. They interact, as cycles do. Generational turnover becomes the mechanism through which populations respond to a shifting economic landscape. That response can look like revolution, reinvention, regression, or renaissance.

What feels personal often begins with what is material. Our stories are shaped by what we need, what we lose, and what we're willing to do to get it back.

What Is the Resource Cycle?

At its core, the resource cycle tracks how societies expand, exhaust, and regenerate their material foundations. Unlike the slow-moving, centuries long rise and fall of empires, this cycle moves on a shorter rhythm over a few decades. Roughly every 50 to 60 years, a familiar pattern plays out, as three forces converge: economic momentum, technological innovation, and conflict.

The rhythm tends to unfold in a similar seasonal pattern as the social cycle:

1. **Spark (Spring)**: A new technology or energy source emerges, expanding productivity and profit.
2. **Expansion (Summer)**: That innovation fuels economic growth as labor, capital, and infrastructure scale to meet demand.
3. **Overheating (Fall)**: Over time, the system strains. Debt piles up. Inequality widens. Resources are stretched.

4. **Crisis (Winter)**: Eventually, the system breaks. Recession, revolution, or war sweeps through as pressure releases. Out of the wreckage, a new equilibrium forms, seeded by the next wave of innovation.

This cycle matters because it explains why feast and famine aren't random but rhythmic. Each generation inherits not just wealth and technology, but also the imbalances created by the last expansion. And when those imbalances peak, societies are forced to confront them (sometimes violently).

When viewed this way, history stops looking like a string of "unprecedented" shocks and instead reveals itself as a series of recurring seasons: planting, growth, harvest, and death.

We are living in the late stage of our current resource cycle. The signs are everywhere. Our economic engine strains under its own weight: wages stagnate while debt, inequality, and speculation balloon. Technology is moving faster than our institutions can adapt. AI, biotech, and decentralized networks are rewriting the rules of work, politics, and even identity. Meanwhile, tensions are peaking, and conflicts are being triggered right on time.

All of this points to a familiar place in the pattern: the system has reached saturation. The current resource cycle is tipping into its reset phase, when the ways we produce, distribute, and protect value must be reinvented. This is where economics, technology, and war intertwine, each one revealing how a civilization decides who gets what, and at what cost.

Let's break down these three aspects of the resource cycle to get a better feel for how it works.

What is Socioeconomics

At its core, socioeconomics is about how people organize, distribute, and control resources. It's not an abstract system of charts and numbers; it's the lived reality of how we exchange value to meet our needs. Whether buying a home, paying wages, or purchasing bread, every transaction links one person's spending to another's income. Because humans require food, water, shelter, and security to survive, we are all inherently and inescapably part of the economy.

But what we call "the economy" is more than just charts and numbers. It's a cultural nervous system. A mirror of collective energy, appetite, and belief. And like all living systems, it doesn't move in straight lines. It cycles, driven by waves of innovation, investment, consumption, and, eventually, exhaustion.

Every 50 or so years, the existing policies go from creating growth to causing harm. An economic, political, and cultural crisis emerges. Because we cannot fix our problems with the tools that created it, we are forced to create a radically different approach to resolve it. New leaders rise, new values gain traction, and a new socioeconomic arc begins.

Most of us are familiar with the concept of economic cycles at the micro level. We know them as business cycles, the familiar booms and busts every 5–10 years. We are more comfortable with these shorter ones because we live through them over and over again. But at the macro level, longer arcs are unfolding at the same time. These are the ones that feel unfamiliar or unprecedented and scary. Not because they are, but because they are *to us* since we only live through each season once or twice in a lifetime.

Here are a few economic cycles you might have heard of:

- **Kitchin cycles (~3–5 years):** driven by inventory fluctuations and short-term business adjustments.

- **Juglar cycles (~7–11 years):** centered on business investment and fixed capital formation.
- **Kuznets cycles (~15–25 years):** linked to infrastructure, housing, and demographic shifts.
- ***Kondratieff waves (~50–60 years):** shaped by technological revolutions and long-term innovation patterns.
- ***Long-Term Debt Cycles (~75–100 years):** governed by the rise and collapse of credit systems.

*The last two are the ones we will be focusing on in this book.

No matter the timescale, the point is the same: economies move in patterns. Beneath the day-to-day noise of inflation numbers and market swings is a deeper rhythm that shapes how prosperity rises, plateaus, and falls.

Kondratieff Waves: The Long Rhythm of Capitalism

The first known theory about modern cyclical economies came in the early 20th century, when two Dutch economists, Jacob van Gelderen and Salomon de Wolff, suggested that capitalist economies might run on 50–60 year rhythms.

However, it was the Soviet economist Nikolai Kondratieff (1892–1938) who brought the idea into public focus. In 1926, he published *The Major Economic Cycles*, arguing that modern economies don't simply grow in straight lines but experience predictable arcs of expansion, plateau, and decline. His reward for pointing this out under Stalin? Arrest, exile to Siberia, and eventually death in the gulag. Thankfully his work outlived him, becoming a cornerstone for long-wave economic theory and earning his name a permanent place in economic history.

Today, these patterns are known as Kondratieff waves (or K-waves, supercycles, or long waves). Each wave lasts roughly 40 to 60 years and contains three broad phases: expansion, stagnation, and recession. Later theorists began to describe them in "seasons": spring (growth), summer (inflation), fall (debt expansion), and winter (deflation and crisis).

Like most cycles, K-waves aren't exact in timing but their rhythm is unmistakable. They show up as long pulses of innovation, growth, and collapse, shaping both economies and societies.

The first documented Kondratiev Wave began around 1790, driven by two inventions that transformed production: the steam engine and the mechanical loom. Together, they launched the Industrial Revolution and ignited decades of economic expansion. By 1815, that initial surge had reached its peak. Growth slowed, markets became saturated, and the cycle turned downward.

During the downswing, the groundwork for the next wave quietly formed. Between 1825 and 1847, a cluster of breakthrough inventions appeared, including the public steam railway, turbine, Portland cement, mechanical harvester, telegraph, rotary printing press, and sewing machine. These innovations fueled the second Kondratiev Wave, beginning around 1850, when railways and telegraphs redefined communication, mobility, and trade. For nearly twenty-five years, economies boomed until the speculative railway bubble burst in 1873, triggering a prolonged global downturn known as the Long Depression.

By the 1890s, a new technological foundation had emerged: electricity. Alongside the assembly line, electrification revolutionized production and ushered in the third Kondratiev Wave. Modern mass production and consumer culture took shape. When Russian economist Nikolai Kondratiev published his findings in 1926, he argued that each long wave of economic growth would inevitably reach a limit and decline. Three years later, the

Great Depression proved his point.

Initially overlooked, Kondratiev's theory gained attention when Austrian economist Joseph Schumpeter expanded on it in *Business Cycles* (1939), framing these long waves as driven by clusters of innovation and creative destruction. Though controversial at first, the concept became one of the cornerstones of innovation theory.

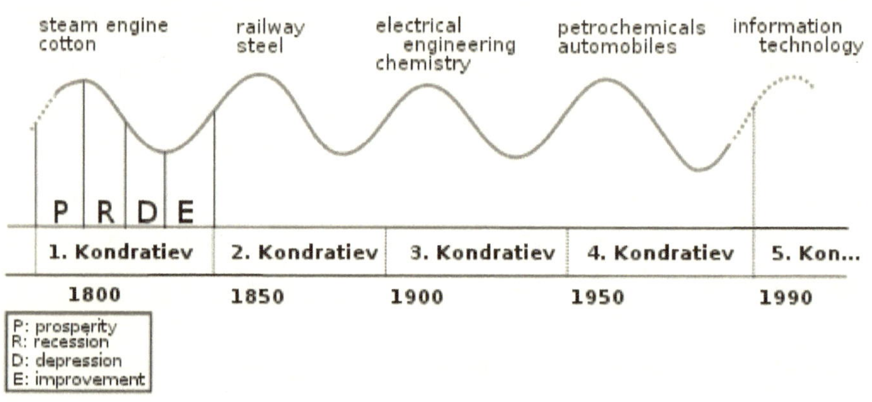

The fourth Kondratiev Wave began in the mid-1940s, powered by oil, automobiles, and aviation. For more than three decades, "individual mobility" defined the global economy. But the oil crises of the 1970s marked the end of that cycle and the beginning of another transition. The fifth, and current, wave took shape in the 1980s with the rise of information technology. Computers became mainstream, the Internet connected the world, and mobile phones transformed communication. As before, rapid growth led to overextension. The dot-com crash of 2001 signaled the crest and beginning of the end for that wave.

Since then, economists and futurists have pointed to the emergence of a sixth Kondratiev Wave, centered on sustainability, biotechnology, and health. Based on typical cycle length and indicators, it looks like Spring is right around the corner.

Since the Industrial Revolution, these K-waves have appeared again and again, each one shaped by a new technological breakthrough:

- Steam and textiles in the late 1700s
- Railroads and steel in the 1800s
- Electricity and chemicals in the early 1900s
- Automobiles and oil in the mid-20th century
- Information technology and the internet in the late 20th century
- And now, an emerging wave built on AI, renewable energy, and decentralized systems.

K-waves help us zoom out. They remind us that today's turbulence is the end of one era and the beginning of another. Each wave follows the same rhythm of expansion, saturation, and reset. It's the heartbeat of capitalism, repeating itself every few generations.

The Saturn-Uranus Cycle

Just as Pluto gave us another lens and language to examine generations, the Saturn-Uranus cycle gives us another (perhaps even more accurate way) to look at the K-wave.

Saturn rules structures, institutions, and stability, while Uranus demands disruption, rebellion, and liberation. When they align, square, or oppose each other in the sky every forty to fifty years, the tension between preservation and revolution breaks open into collective life. What's interesting is how closely this rhythm mirrors the Kondratiev waves of economics. Both tell the same story in different languages. A K-wave begins with a "spring" of new inventions and expansion, overheats into "summer" conflict, matures into an "autumn" of speculation and instability, and crashes into a "winter" of depression and restructuring before the next wave begins.

Saturn–Uranus maps the same pattern: conjunction as innovation, opposition as confrontation, waning square as crisis, and the next conjunction as rebirth.

- **Conjunction (0°):** The start of the cycle — new systems and innovations are seeded.
- **First square (~10–11 years later):** Tension builds as change pushes against established order.
- **Opposition (~20–22 years in):** The cycle reaches full polarity — revolution vs. tradition.
- **Final square (~33–36 years in):** Crisis, reform, or collapse of outdated structures.
- **Next conjunction (~44–46 years):** A new cycle begins.

U.S. history bears this out. Two cycles ago, the 1942 conjunction in Taurus coincided with World War II and the wartime restructuring that launched the long postwar boom and the "spring" of a new order. By the opposition in the 1960s, Civil Rights, counterculture, and Vietnam protests tore at the fabric of the old system bringing the heat of "summer." The waning square of the 1970s mirrored K-wave autumn: stagflation, Watergate, oil shocks, and deep disillusionment.

The 1988–89 conjunction brought "winter into spring," as the Soviet Union collapsed while America entered the digital and financial age. A new cycle started. At the opposition of 2008–10, the Great Recession and populist uprisings revealed a system cracking apart. And in 2021, Saturn and Uranus clashed again in square, just as the world reeled from a pandemic, protests, and widening polarization (a true K-wave winter) as old structures buckle under digital disruption, inequality, and crisis.

Comparison of Saturn–Uranus Cycles and K-Waves

Period	Saturn–Uranus Phase	Approx. Dates	Kondratiev Wave Phase	Approx. Dates
1st Industrial Era	Conjunction (steam/industrial dawn)	1791–1793	*1st K-Wave*: Steam & Textiles (Expansion)	~1780–1845
	Opposition (railway revolutions)	1819–1821	Peak / Overheating	~1810–1830
	Waning Square (industrial adjustment)	1834–1836	Decline / Recession	~1830–1845
Railway & Steel Age	Conjunction	1852–1853	*2nd K-Wave*: Railroads & Steel	~1845–1896
	Opposition	1875–1877	Peak / Crisis (Long Depression)	~1873–1896
	Waning Square	1897–1899	End of Cycle	~1890s
Electricity & Mass Production	Conjunction	1897–1899	*3rd K-Wave*: Electricity & Chemicals	~1896–1945
	Opposition	1918–1920	Peak / Overheating (WWI–Roaring 20s)	~1910–1930
	Waning Square	1930–1931	Crisis / Great Depression	~1930s
Automobile & Oil Age	Conjunction	1942	*4th K-Wave*: Automobiles & Oil	~1945–1973
	Opposition	1965–1967	Peak / Social Upheaval	~1960–1970
	Waning Square	1975–1977	Crisis / Stagflation	~1970–1980
Digital & Information Age	Conjunction	1988–1989	*5th K-Wave*: Information Technology	~1980–2008
	Opposition	2008–2010	Crisis / Financial Collapse	~2008–2010
	Waning Square	2021	K-Wave "Winter" / Reset	~2020s
AI, Biotech & Decentralized Systems	**Next Conjunction (Projected)**	**2032–2035**	**6th K-Wave: Human & Environmental Tech (Spring)**	**~2030–2080**

As you can see in the chart the dates of the K-wave and Saturn-Uranus aspects differ slightly, but the major conjunctions and oppositions consistently align with innovation booms, wars, crises, and economic turning points.

The impending conjunction in the early 2030s signals the beginning of a new K-wave. The last time Saturn and Uranus met at a conjunction, in 1988–89, the world watched the fall of the Berlin Wall, the unraveling of the Cold War order, and the birth of the digital age. The time before that, in 1942, the U.S. was remaking itself through wartime mobilization, laying the foundation for the postwar boom of becoming a world superpower. In the early 2030s, we should expect something on that scale: the obvious collapse of institutions and systems that no longer serve and the solidification of new systems built on today's disruptive technologies. Perhaps it will be artificial intelligence, biotechnology, decentralized finance, green energy, and/or global networks. Or it may be something we can't even see yet and only seems obvious in retrospect. If the past cycles hold true, the lead up to the mid 2030s will feel like a harsh but necessary reset, when the old ways finally give way to something dramatically new. For the United States, this may mean constitutional reform, new economic foundations, and a reframing of its role in the world. For the globe, it likely marks the dawn of a wave of prosperity born out of the crucible of the 2020s.

* * *

A Short & Sweet History of Economic Thought

Economics is essentially the way humans decide to deal with resources—how we gather, share, and use them. Like all human inventions, no single approach holds the truth forever. Economic theories tend to arise in response to the challenges of their time, offering new ways to solve old problems until the cycle shifts again. Over the centuries ideas resurface in new forms under different conditions, never identical, but always familiar.

The first major system of the modern era was Mercantilism (1500–1776). Born from the rise of nation-states and overseas exploration, it saw wealth as fixed and scarce. Gold and silver were hoarded, colonies were exploited, and exports were valued over imports. Nationalism, militarism, and colonization flourished under mercantilism, laying the foundation for global capitalism. Its logic persists today in practices like offshoring and protectionist trade policies.

60

In 1776, Classical economics emerged with Adam Smith's Wealth of Nations. Smith and his contemporaries emphasized free markets, private property, and minimal government interference, arguing that individuals pursuing their own interests would serve the greater good—the famous "invisible hand." This era coincided with the Industrial Revolution: factories, enclosure laws, and cheap labor transformed society, fueling growth but also deepening inequality. Smith himself warned against the corruption of moral sentiment that comes when wealth and power are admired more than wisdom or virtue.

By the 19th century, industrialization had created misery alongside progress. Socialism arose as a countercurrent, advocating state intervention, worker protections, and social programs. Many of the labor laws and social safety nets we now take for granted were once radical socialist proposals. Later, the Great Depression of the 1930s paved the way for Keynesian economics, which argued that governments must actively manage demand through spending, taxation, and monetary policy. This approach shaped much of the 20th century, particularly the postwar boom. Today, mainstream economics blends neoclassical microeconomics with Keynesian-inspired macroeconomics—an uneasy hybrid still evolving as new crises demand new theories.

The lesson? Economic thought is never static. No framework is a straight line toward truth or finality, but a tool of adaptation, contradiction, and reinvention.

* * *

Technology as the Spark

The more conventional explanation for what signals a new K-wave is a technological breakthrough that shifts what is possible on a fundamental level. These sparks ignite revolutions not only in industry but in identity. They rewire how we live, what we value, and what we believe about the future. If economics is the system that organizes value, technology is the force that redefines it. Each breakthrough changes the game: what counts as wealth, who controls it, and how it is distributed.

Most cycle theorists today follow what's known as the Schumpeter–Freeman–Perez paradigm, which identifies five completed technological waves since the Industrial Revolution, and a sixth now emerging:

1. **The Industrial Revolution (1771):** Steam engines and mechanized textiles.
2. **The Age of Steam and Railways (1829):** Iron, coal, canals, and rail networks.
3. **The Age of Steel, Electricity, and Heavy Engineering (1875):** Chemicals, machinery, electrotechnics.
4. **The Age of Oil and the Automobile (1908):** Mass production, suburbanization, global wars.
5. **The Age of Information and Telecommunications (1971):** Microchips, computers, and digital networks.

You'll notice the dates of these paradigms precede the beginning of a new K-wave by about a decade each time. This is because the technology that really kicks off the new K-wave is founded in the winter of the previous cycle. Under this framework, each wave made life faster, more connected, and seemingly more efficient. But each also introduced new forms of dislocation, inequality, and control. Technology doesn't just solve problems, it also creates new ones that force adaptation, often before we understand what we've agreed to.

And right now, we are entering another leap. Artificial intelligence is beginning to automate thought itself, reshaping how knowledge is created, organized, and applied. Quantum computing is emerging just behind it, promising to solve problems that lie far beyond the reach of today's machines. Renewable energy technologies are redefining the foundations of power (literally and geopolitically) as nations race to secure dominance in a shifting geopolitical order. Meanwhile, blockchain and decentralized networks are rewriting the rules of trust, ownership, and exchange. And as augmented and virtual realities advance, the line between the real and the rendered grows thinner, pulling human experience into an entirely new dimension. The transformation underway is not only changing what we can do, but what it means to be human.

All that being said, the rhythm is still familiar. Innovation sparks production, growth, and the spring of a new cycle. Technology makes it easier and faster to extract and distribute resources. Industries emerge, businesses thrive, markets boom, and inflation rises in the summer of expansion. Then comes autumn when growth slows, debt builds, inequality widens. Finally, winter is marked by crisis, collapse, and war, resetting the cycle and forcing new rules on the game.

If past waves were defined in retrospect by single breakthroughs (steam, rail, oil, microchips), our era is marked by a constellation of overlapping technologies. Only time will tell which one(s) are the primary movers.

- **Artificial intelligence** is automating cognition itself, shifting value from human expertise to machine learning models.
- **Quantum computing** promises to crack problems—from encryption to drug discovery—that classical machines can't touch.
- **Renewable energy systems** (solar, wind, storage, smart grids) are rewiring geopolitics by making energy more localized and abundant.
- **Blockchain and decentralized networks** are challenging how we store, verify, and exchange value, potentially eroding the power of centralized financial systems.
- **Augmented and virtual realities** are dissolving the line between physical and digital, making presence, identity, and even reality itself a contested resource.

This is more than a wave of new gadgets. It is a massive shift in what counts as value, who controls it, and how it flows. For the first time, the "resource" being extracted at scale is not coal or oil, but us: our attention, our behavior, our data.

Human consciousness has become a business model.

That shift destabilizes the entire socioeconomic order. Factories give way to platforms. Wages give way to equity. Tangible output gives way to metrics (likes, clicks, follows, etc.). The new extraction is ambient, invisible, and constant. We are working all the time without realizing it, simply by being online, producing the data and narratives that fuel the system.

The labor market is already seeing destabilization that will only continue to grow. Work is being unbundled and redefined: from hands to minds, from visible production to invisible participation. Careers feel precarious, caught between automation and constant reskilling. What used to feel like a path now feels like a moving target in a rigged carnival game.

Institutions struggle even more. The metrics we rely on like GDP, jobs, or inflation were built for an industrial world of goods and wages. They lag behind digital realities where much of the "work" is unpaid or uncounted and more of the "wealth" is beginning to exist in intangible assets like data or intellectual property. Schools, governments, and regulators move too slowly to set guardrails, while technology accelerates on a quarterly cadence. This mismatch naturally breeds an instability we can all feel.

As with any new technology, the double edge is clear. These tools can democratize access or centralize control. They can empower creation or deepen addiction. They collapse old orders and open new paradigms, but not without turbulence, inequality, and dislocation along the way. The task is not to romanticize or demonize them but remember they are mirrors of the consciousness that made them.

America's Socioeconomic Cycles

As a quick case study, let's look apply the socioeconomic cycle to America.

In his book *The Storm Before the Calm*, geopolitical analyst George Friedman identifies five major socioeconomic eras in U.S. history. Each cycle lasts roughly 50–60 years and ends in crisis, forcing the country to reinvent both its economy and its governing philosophy. These loosely line up with K-waves and Saturn-Uranus conjunctions.

- **Washington Cycle (1783–1828)**: The founding era. America was a young, agrarian republic built on decentralized power and local governance. The central tension was between unity and autonomy and figuring out how to hold a nation together without becoming the monarchy it had just escaped.
- **Jackson Cycle (1828–1876)**: The age of expansion and democratization. Industrialization began reshaping the economy while the moral and political crisis of slavery tore the country apart. This cycle ended violently with the Civil War and Reconstruction, as the question of federal versus state power reached a breaking point.
- **Hayes Cycle (1876–1929)**: The rise of industrial capitalism. Railroads, steel, oil, and mass immigration transformed America into a global industrial power. Wealth concentrated at the top while workers organized at the bottom. The Gilded Age created extraordinary growth but also deep inequality, setting the stage for the Great Depression.
- **Roosevelt Cycle (1932–1980)**: The New Deal and postwar era. Out of economic collapse came a reimagined social contract. The federal government expanded to regulate markets, provide welfare, and manage global leadership through the Second World War and the Cold War. Prosperity was broad-based, but centralization came at a cost: bureaucracy, stagnation, and dependence on state power.
- **Reagan Cycle (1981–2030?)**: The neoliberal era. Deregulation, tax reform, and globalization dismantled much of the New Deal system.

Manufacturing gave way to finance and technology, while digital networks reshaped communication and commerce. The rise of markets as moral arbiters fueled growth and innovation but hollowed out the middle class. Wealth pooled in fewer hands, and the institutions built in the mid-20th century began to fracture under the weight of inequality and distrust.

Our current socioeconomic cycle began in 1981 with the Reagan era, a turning point that redefined markets, government, and power itself. Deregulation and tax reform reshaped industries, while globalization and digitization extended American influence across the world. Finance replaced manufacturing as the engine of growth, and speculation became a national pastime. This shift was fueled by the collapse of what had once been the backbone of American society: industrial labor.

During this cycle, abundant money and low interest rates made credit easy to access but failed to generate truly productive investment. Capital flowed into real estate and financial markets instead of innovation or infrastructure, driving up asset prices and shutting out those without existing wealth. The result is the world we see today: housing out of reach, wages stagnant, and institutions gridlocked under the weight of their own design.

By the late 2000s that model began to stall. Now, as we approach 2030, the cycle is nearing turnover. The system still functions enough, but only through momentum. In this late stage, perception often outweighs production as attention, narrative, and hype become currencies as powerful as money itself.

Every cycle begins with optimism and vows of new policies, new elites, and new values promising life will get better. But in time, the very systems built to stabilize society become rigid and brittle under their own success. Economic pain follows, then political instability, and finally contempt as each side is convinced the other is to blame. By default, each cycle ends in failure.

This is how every era ends: not with a single villain, but with a system outgrowing its own design. The collapse isn't anyone's evil or idiotic plan, or even an accident. It's structural. The natural reset of an economic cycle that has run its course.

History shows the pattern clearly. The industrial expansion that followed the Civil War lasted from the 1870s to the 1920s, driven by railroads, steel, electrification, and urban growth. By its end, debt outpaced productivity, inequality soared, and speculation detached from reality. The Great Depression of the 1930s was the inevitable winter of that wave. Out of its ashes came the postwar boom—the Bretton Woods order of 1944, powered by the dollar, reconstruction, and mass consumerism. That system carried growth until the 1970s before breaking down, paving the way for the neoliberal era of the 1980s.

Today, the growth-at-all-costs model that powered the previous era is running on fumes. Since the 2008 financial crisis, the global economy has been propped up by artificially low interest rates, speculative bubbles, and historic debt. We've stretched the endgame into overtime, but extension is not evolution. The reckoning simply grows larger because debt is more than just a measurement of money, it's energetic. When we borrow beyond our means, whether in money, time, attention, or ecology, balance eventually demands restoration. And when correction comes, it never feels comfortable.

Cycles in the Price of Commodities

In his book Cycles: The Science of Prediction (1947), Edward R. Dewey (chief economist of the U.S. Department of Commerce during the early 1930s) argued that business cycles often begin not with governments or corporations, but with consumers. Every time you make a major purchase—whether buying a home, trading in your car, or stocking up on groceries—you're making a quiet prediction about the future price of that item.

Will housing prices rise or fall? Should you wait for the seasonal discount? Corporations play this forecasting game too when they launch products or time investments in hopes of catching the best price environment. Prices may appear to be driven by supply and demand, tariffs, inflation, or currency fluctuations. But beneath those obvious forces lies a deeper rhythm.

Since World War II, prices have climbed to ever-higher plateaus, yet even in their upward march they've fluctuated in repeating rises and falls that can't be fully explained by classical economics. Dewey wasn't the first one to notice this of course. In the book of Genesis, Joseph interpreted Pharaoh's dream of seven fat cows devoured by seven lean cows as a prophecy of seven years of plenty followed by seven years of famine. His advice to store grain during the fat years was one of the earliest recorded recognitions that resource cycles follow a predictable rhythm.

Centuries later, a bankrupt hog and corn farmer named Samuel Benner took up the same advice. After losing everything in the Panic of 1873, he began charting commodity prices. By 1875, he had discovered regular cycles in pig iron, cotton, wheat, and pork prices, and even an 18-year rhythm in economic panics. His book "Benner's Prophecies or Future Ups and Downs in Prices" (1876) became one of the first attempts to map these economic ups and downs.

Remarkably, had you traded pig iron according to Benner's cycle between 1875 and 1935, you would have profited forty-four times more than you lost. His timing was slightly off after 1935, but not because the pattern disappeared, but because the true rhythm was 9.2 years instead of the 9 he had calculated.

The lesson: markets are not random and prices, like people, follow patterns of expansion and contraction that repeat across generations.

We are living in the end of one cycle, but we can also catch glimpses of what might be over the horizon. Old industries cling to relevance, new ones rush to maturity, and people are left disoriented in the gap between. This overlap explains the volatility we feel daily. Jobs feel precarious, institutions incoherent, and narratives fractured because the rules of the old game no longer apply, but the rules of the new one haven't been written. Our politics reflect this tension: distrust, division, and a gnawing sense that no one is really in control.

The tools we are building right now, the seeds of the next K-wave, are not neutral; they are mirrors of the consciousness that made them. And as Marshall McLuhan reminded us: *we shape our tools, and then our tools shape us.* Right now, our tools are moving faster than our institutions, faster than our cultural norms, faster than our nervous systems. When that happens, pressure builds. Inequality spikes. Narratives collapse. Trust erodes. And eventually, the system demands a reset.

Human survival has always been tied to controlling resources, and the tighter we feel they are getting, the fiercer the competition becomes. That competition doesn't stop at the marketplace. It spills into politics, militaries, and treaties. And this is what ushers in the third force of the resource cycle: war.

4

War & Climate Cycles

Cycle Length	Varies; but ~50-100 years*
Featured Cycles	<ul><li>17.7-year war cycle</li><li>53.5 year "major" war cycle</li><li>~100 year "general" war cycle</li><li>Saturn-Pluto Cycle</li><li>Solar cycle</li><li>~100-year climate cycle</li></ul>
Next Cycle (approx.)	Late 2020s-2060/80s
Key Themes of War & Climate Cycle	<ul><li>Tension accumulation</li><li>Trigger event</li><li>Restructuring of power</li><li>Amnesia ("never again")</li><li>*Mirrors Socioeconomic (50 years) & Institutional cycles (100 years)</li></ul>

Every socioeconomic cycle eventually hits a wall. Growth slows. Debt piles up. Technology destabilizes more than it solves. And beneath the surface, pressure builds. When economic models falter and innovations upend the social order, that pressure doesn't simply dissolve. It concentrates. And historically, it has almost always found its release through war.

War is both a driver and a consequence of resource cycles. As nations compete for access, scarcity, or dominance, conflict becomes the crude reset button. Major wars redraw power maps, collapse old institutions, and force a reallocation of resources. They are horrific, yet they serve a structural function: clearing the field when other systems can no longer adapt.

This is not just theory. In the past 3,400 years, humanity has known little more than 200 years of true peace. Wars appear to erupt from single sparks—the assassination of Archduke Ferdinand in 1914, the invasion of Poland in 1939, the toppling of the Twin Towers in 2001—but these sparks ignite only because tinder has already accumulated.

War is never random. It is the delayed response of pressures that have been building for years, even decades. Patterns of conflict repeat with remarkable regularity, echoing the same rhythms that govern credit and innovation. To see war as purely chaotic is to miss the deeper rhythm: a grim but measurable pulse in history's body.

War Cycles

If war seems chaotic, history suggests otherwise. Conflict loosely follows rhythms just as economies do. Scholars from Quincy Wright to Arnold Toynbee to modern cycle theorists have found that wars emerge in strikingly regular intervals, echoing the same long waves that govern innovation and credit.

Edward Dewey's analysis of Raymond Wheeler's War Index, which tracks conflicts from 600 B.C. to 1950 A.D., showed that wars tend to cluster at regular intervals rather than occur randomly. Across 2,500 years of data, it became clear that there were consistent rhythms in the outbreak of war and when certain cycles overlap, their effects amplify. Smaller oscillations often stack on top of larger ones, creating "eras of general war" followed by quieter periods of recovery and reorganization. That's why certain moments in history—1776 to 1783, 1861 to 1865, 1914 to 1918, and now 2020 to

2030—feel especially charged. Multiple cycles are cresting at once, creating turbulence that extends across politics, economics, and culture.

While there are multiple war cycles we could focus on (like the multiple economic cycles), two war sub-cycles repeat most consistently:

- **The 8.8-year cycle:** often tied to flare-ups, proxy wars, or military escalations.
- **The 17.7-year cycle:** often coinciding with peak involvement in larger conflicts.

Together, two 8.8 sub-cycles form a 17.7 year cycle, and three 17.7 cycles form a 53.5-year major war cycle, which alternates between smaller regional wars and larger "total wars." Over two cycles—roughly 100 years—we see the institutional cycle turn over and a new saeculum begin, often coinciding with a "general" war. (More on this in chapter 5).

The 17.7-Year War Cycle

Not all wars are world wars. Many conflicts break out in shorter rhythms that are just as measurable. Two of these are the 8.8-year and the 17.7-year war cycles.

The shorter 8.8-year cycle often marks flare-ups: regional conflicts, escalations, or proxy wars that set the stage for larger confrontations. They are like the building blocks that set the stage over time. The 17.7-year cycle (or approximately every other 8.8 cycle) is more consequential. It aligns closely with economic and biological cycles and has been documented as far back as 600 BC. This rhythm doesn't just appear in the timing of wars but also aligns with economic cycles like U.S. wholesale prices, Nile flood stages, and commodity markets (all pointing to its deep roots in the balance of resources). This minor war cycle tends to align with domestic unrest

Looking specifically at this cycle applied to America, the pattern is impressive. Counting forward in 17.7-year cycles from Lexington and Concord in 1775, U.S. involvement peaks consistently line up:

1775 — War of Independence

Birth of the United States through armed revolt; military action becomes the origin myth of the nation.

1793 — Whiskey Rebellion

First deployment of federal military force against U.S. citizens; sets precedent for internal militarized federal authority.

1812 — War of 1812

U.S. declares war on Britain; national identity forged through external conflict and defense of sovereignty.

1829 — Jacksonian Era / Indian Removal Doctrine

Military-backed forced relocation of Indigenous peoples; expansionist conflict becomes state policy.

1846–1848 — Mexican–American War

U.S. invades Mexico and annexes vast territory; continental empire-building through war.

1863 — Civil War Apex

Battles of Gettysburg and Vicksburg mark peak of internal war; total war strategy emerges on American soil.

1881 — Apache Wars / Final Indian Wars + Domestic Anarchist Tension

Last major Indigenous resistance suppressed; assassination of President

Garfield sparks militarized policing mentality.

1898–1899 — Spanish–American War & Philippine–American War
U.S. becomes an overseas imperial power; colonial acquisition begins beyond the continent.

1916–1917 — World War I Entry
Selective Service Act introduces mass conscription; the modern national war machine is born.

1934–1936 — Pre-WWII Rearmament and Internal Coup Attempt
Bonus Army protests, Business Plot coup attempt, and economic militarization signal internal and external war posturing.

1951–1952 — Korean War Escalation
U.S. enters direct combat with communist forces; Cold War military architecture solidifies.

1968–1969 — Vietnam War Peak + Domestic Insurrection
Tet Offensive, draft resistance, riots, and civil unrest mark simultaneous external and internal war pressure.

1985–1986 — Reagan Doctrine Proxy Wars
U.S. funds global insurgencies in Nicaragua, Afghanistan, and beyond; Cold War conflict outsourced globally.

2001–2003 — 9/11 and the War on Terror
U.S. invades Afghanistan and Iraq; Patriot Act launches the surveillance state and permanent war footing.

2020–2022 — Afghanistan Withdrawal Collapse + Ukraine & Middle East Escalations
End of 20-year war collides with rapid emergence of new global conflict

blocs; public language shifts toward "WWIII structure."

~2039–2040 (Projected)

Uranus in Gemini + Pluto in Aquarius = historical war signatures repeat; analysts speculate a major global conflict inflection involving reorganized alliances and technological warfare.

Of course, this cycle doesn't always manifest as an official declaration of war. Sometimes it shows up as internal militarization, regime stress, or foreign build-ups. But every ~17.7 years, the United States reaches a new threshold of conflict engagement or military identity realignment.

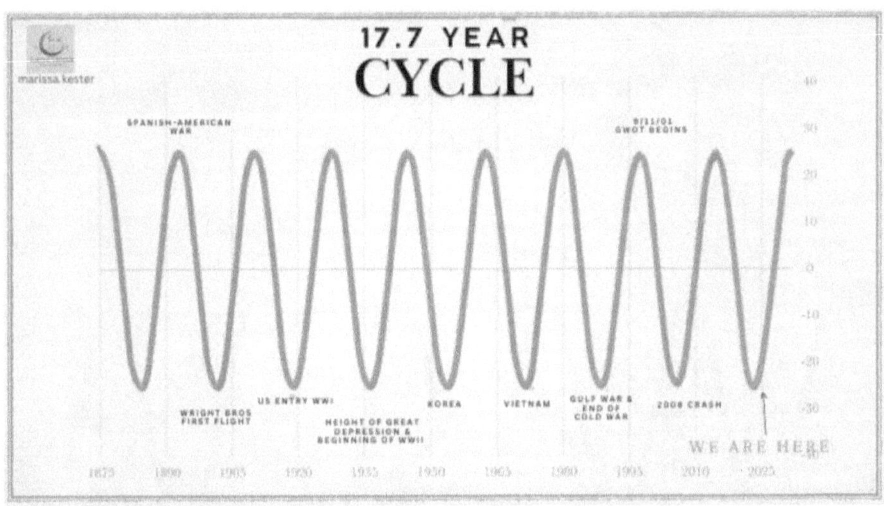

Major War Cycle: 53.5 Years

Three cycles of 17.7 years add up to roughly 53.5 years, or the length of the "major" war cycle. These cycles function as nested patterns, with the shorter 8.8- and 17.7-year oscillations building into larger systemic resets about every half century.

Looking at war from this cyclical perspective, we can see that the 53–54-year major war cycle often runs in sync with socioeconomic waves. Global conflicts seem to erupt at the climax of resource strain, when societies can no longer expand through trade, growth, or invention and begin turning against each other instead. Wars, in this sense, are not random but act as the release valve of a system under pressure.

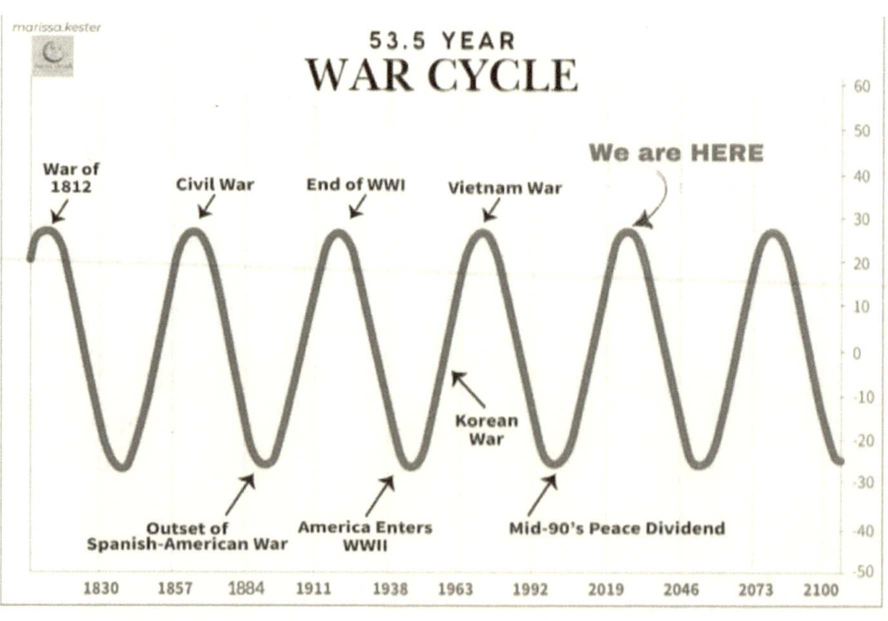

The 53.5-year Major War Cycle is often attributed to the work of Quincy Wright (alongside complementary analysis by Edward R. Dewey at the Foundation for the Study of Cycles). Wright identified a recurring 53–54-year rhythm between peaks of major international wars, particularly in the European and later global system.

Using Wright's baseline (circa 1495–1501 as the start of modern state warfare with the Italian Wars) and applying the 53.5-year rhythm, the major war peaks align approximately with:

- **1495–1501:** Italian Wars begin, marking the birth of modern state warfare.
- **1548–1554:** Religious conflicts escalate across Europe (Schmalkaldic War fallout, French tensions rise).
- **1602–1608:** Conditions build toward the Thirty Years' War (Dutch Revolt tensions peak).
- **1655–1661:** Anglo-Spanish War, Northern Wars, broad European militarization.
- **1708–1714:** War of Spanish Succession, often considered the first truly global imperial conflict.
- **1761–1767:** Seven Years' War resolution, sometimes referred to as the first real world war.
- **1814–1820:** Napoleonic Wars climax and the Congress of Vienna restructures Europe.
- **1867–1873:** Franco-Prussian War, unification of Germany, and U.S. post–Civil War militarization.
- **1920–1926:** Aftermath of World War I, rise of fascism, and global tensions that set the stage for World War II.
- **1973–1979:** Middle East wars, Vietnam endgame, Cold War flashpoints, and oil shocks.
- **2026–2032 (Projected):** Expected great power realignment, AI and cyber warfare, currency and resource conflicts, and systemic geopolitical

restructuring.

Based on the 53.5 year major way cycle (which again, is roughly three 17.7 year cycles), we can reasonably expect that the correct conditions exist for conflict and military escalation in the late 2020s. This does not mean war has to play out a certain way, or will necessarily even play out with physical violence. We could see trade wars, diplomatic wars, or this release valve function in a more sub-surface kind of way. Remember, cycles don't *cause* wars or recessions, they simply create probability windows when conditions are ripe for conflict.

While this 53.5-year rhythm points to recurring peaks in conflict intensity, there is a century-long war cycle that drives the smaller ones. In his *Study of War*, Quincy Wright observed that wars tend to recur in "50-year oscillations, each alternate period of concentration being more severe." British historian Arnold Toynbee made similar observations, identifying a major systemic reset about every 95 years. Both linked this rhythm to generational experience: one cycle after a decisive war, the memory fades, and a new generation leads nations back into conflict. It's the old adage in action: *hard times make strong men, strong men make good times, good times make weak men, weak men make hard times. (aka the Saeculum).*

These "systemic wars" do more than escalate violence; they reset the world order itself, redrawing borders, rewriting laws, and installing new financial and political architectures that define the next age. The approximate peaks of the 100 year general war cycle are:

- **~1500s**: Italian Wars and the rise of nation-state warfare in Europe; marks the beginning of organized interstate military systems.
- **~1618–1648**: Thirty Years' War; religious and dynastic conflict that reshaped Europe and ended with the Peace of Westphalia.

- **~1700–1715**: War of Spanish Succession; redistribution of imperial power and colonial territories.
- **~1792–1815**: French Revolutionary and Napoleonic Wars; collapse of monarchic order and reshaping of Europe under new ideological systems.
- **~1914–1945**: World War I and World War II (understood as one extended systemic war); destruction of empires and birth of the American-led world order.
- **~2030–2050 (Projected)**: Anticipated systemic conflict and reorganization of global power structure during the AI/Biotech/Climate resource warfare era.

In this view, war is not random chaos but a kind of collective pressure release built into the larger rhythm of civilization. America's wars, from the Revolution to the Civil War to the World Wars and beyond, follow this same pulse almost mathematically.

History doesn't repeat mechanically, but energy does build in waves until it demands expression. The wars we fight, then, are less about isolated events and more about the turning of a larger wheel, one that appears to be spinning toward another crest in the 2020s and 2030s.

The Saturn-Pluto Cycle

Roughly every 33 to 38 years, Saturn (structure, limits, law, and material reality) and Pluto (power, death, transformation) meet either next to one another, or opposite the wheel from one another (conjunction or opposition). When this particular relationship occurs, it gets heavy. The Saturn-Pluto cycle is known for humanity's most difficult trials: genocide, ethnocide, epidemics, mass killings, and the like. These are periods of contraction, crisis, and conservative reaction when the old order tightens its grip.

Here are a few notable examples:

- **1348–1351**: Their conjunction coincided with the Black Death, the pandemic that shattered medieval Europe and birthed the Renaissance.
- **1914–1915**: Another conjunction marked the outbreak of World War I, the death of empires, and the beginning of modernity.
- **1931–1939**: Their opposition and subsequent conjunction framed the Great Depression and the rise of totalitarian regimes, culminating in World War II.
- **1982–1983**: Another conjunction coincided with the AIDS epidemic, the height of the Cold War, and the dawn of neoliberal globalization.
- **2001–2002**: Their opposition aligned with 9/11 and the subsequent War on Terror.
- **2019–2020**: The most recent conjunction brought COVID-19, global lockdowns, and cultural division.

Saturn governs law, justice, duty, labor, and material reality. It represents time itself and the awareness of our limited time in this physical experience. Pluto rules death, destruction, and regeneration. When they align, Saturn's impulse to define meets Pluto's impulse to annihilate. Together, they press civilizations to the edge, exposing what has decayed and forcing transformation through necessity rather than inspiration.

Astrologer Richard Tarnas calls these alignments "periods of profoundly weighty events of enduring consequence." They evoke a collective sense that life is being shaped by vast, impersonal forces beyond human control. In response, societies often polarize into the archetypal struggle of *victim versus oppressor,* each side convinced it is the one being constrained or crushed by history.

These periods bring pandemics, wars, and institutional breakdowns, not because the planets "cause" them, but because they mirror the psychological and structural tension of an age reaching its limits.

In the United States' national chart (also known as the Sibly chart), we are still living the effects of the most recent Saturn-Pluto conjunction in 2019-2020. Saturn's recent transit through Pisces and the third house has exposed systemic confusion in media and education, the fog of misinformation, the crisis of trust, the breakdown of shared reality. Pluto's slow crawl through Capricorn and now Aquarius has been excavating the nation's institutional foundations, dragging hidden power structures to the surface.

The Saturn–Pluto cycle transforms through contraction. It forces us to face endings we've postponed. The destruction is rarely sudden; it's slow, grinding, and bureaucratic. Yet in hindsight, these periods always prove pivotal. They are history's pruning phases, cutting away what no longer serves so that something new can eventually grow. The shadow of this cycle is oppression and fear. Its gift is endurance, discipline, and the rebuilding of moral and material foundations.

The current Saturn-Pluto cycle just began again with the 2019–2020 conjunction, amplified by a rare triple alignment with Jupiter, which expanded its reach. The pandemic, mass death, authoritarian resurgence, and restructuring of global systems marked the opening act. This energy will continue to unfold through the mid-2030s, culminating in the next Saturn–Pluto opposition (2035–2036) — a window that, historically, corresponds with major geopolitical realignments and often, global conflict.

From War to Weather

Scholars have long noticed that major wars often coincide with environmental stress: droughts, floods, crop failures, and shifts in solar activity. Data shows that the same 142-year rhythm seen in international conflict also appears in tree rings, river flood stages, and sediment layers across the globe. In other words, the Earth itself seems to pulse in time with human unrest.

When climates shift, resources strain. Harvests fail, migration surges, economies destabilize, and social tension builds. The conditions that make peace possible like abundance, stability, and predictability, begin to erode. Fear takes root. And eventually, that fear finds an outlet, whether through revolution, war, or the quieter violence of societal fracture.

War, then, may be less a purely political event than an environmental symptom. Perhaps it is a collective response to planetary stress and cycles. Some researchers, like Italian chemist Giorgio Piccardi, went so far as to argue that war itself may be linked to mass hysteria or collective combativeness that rises and falls at regular intervals. In his book *The Chemical Basis of Medical Climatology*, Piccardi states that "only by understanding the mechanism which connects him to the earth and the sky will man be able to understand his physical and psychic position in the universe today. In the context of the universe as it is, man will find his natural role."

Seen this way, war is not only political or economic. It is environmental. Climate shifts, solar cycles, and planetary rhythms have long coincided with periods of unrest and conflict. When crops fail, when droughts stretch on, when the sun grows more active, human societies feel the strain. Scarcity breeds fear, fear breeds division, and conflict follows.

Climate Cycles

A few years after the early climate-conflict studies emerged, Raymond Wheeler, a psychology professor at the University of Kansas, undertook one of the most ambitious pattern-tracking projects of the 20th century. He and his research team examined 78 major climate shifts dating back to 2500 BCE, charting how each shift corresponded with war, political upheaval, or cultural flourishing. From this massive dataset, Wheeler identified a repeating climate rhythm averaging around 100 years (sometimes as short as 70, sometimes stretching to 120) which appeared to govern the emotional and political temperature of entire civilizations. He later proposed that this century rhythm was nested within an even larger 510-year supercycle (the same cycle we'll return to in Chapter 6).

Wheeler's work indicated that the 100-year climate cycle could be divided into four distinct phases: "Cold-Dry," followed by "Warm-Wet," then "Warm-Dry," and ending with "Cold-Wet" before restarting. While each phase is present in a cycle, they are not all equal in length.

Cold-Dry

A period marked by rigidity and contraction. Resources tighten, populations become more conservative, and societies focus on preservation and discipline. Cultural tone: austerity, centralization, and moral severity. Often linked with social repression or defensive nationalism, but not yet outright militarized expansion. Previous dates include: 1680-1720; 1840-1870; 1965-1985.

Warm-Wet

This phase brings expansion and optimism. Agriculture and trade flourish, population growth accelerates, and cultural confidence rises. Increased resource abundance leads to outward ambition, exploration, and ideological flourishing. This is often when new utopian movements or reformist energies emerge. Previous dates include: 1720-1760; 1870-1900; 1985-2000.

Warm-Dry *(where we are now)*

The high-risk conflict zone. Heat and drying conditions stress resources, leading to competitive expansion, empire-building, and authoritarian consolidation. Wheeler found this phase correlates with police states, aggressive nationalism, financial speculation, and breakdown of economic systems. Global systems become brittle and prone to explosive wars. Previous dates include: 1760-1815; 1900-1945; 2005-2035 (projected)*

Cold-Wet

A corrective and destabilizing phase. Cooling temperatures and excess moisture lead to crop failures, flooding, disease, and population strain. Rather than empire wars, this period tends to produce domestic unrest, revolution from below, democratic agitation, and internal restructuring. Power fragments, elites are challenged, and social contracts are rewritten. Previous dates include: 1815-1840; 1945-1965; 2035-2055 (projected)

Taken together from the last three chapters, we can start to see how many cycles are lining up. According to various frameworks—socioeconomic cycles, the saeculum, war cycles, climate cycles, planetary influences—we are currently in a tinderbox that is primed for conflict. And our sun could act as the match.

Solar Cycles

Most people picture the Sun as a blazing ball of fire, but it is actually a constantly shifting sphere of charged gas. Its round shape is more an illusion of perspective than a fixed boundary. Beneath that apparent stability, magnetic fields twist and snap, producing solar flares and disturbances that subtly alter the Sun's size and shape.

One of the clearest signs of this magnetic restlessness is the appearance of sunspots, dark regions where magnetic loops push through the solar surface. These spots do not appear randomly; they rise and fall in a rhythmic cycle. Over time, scientists have noticed something strange: as solar activity intensifies, so does human activity. It is as if the nervous system of our star resonates with our own.

These solar disturbances do not stay in space. They release electromagnetic radiation in the form of radio waves, ultraviolet bursts, x-rays, and gamma rays. These emissions travel toward Earth on the solar wind, where they interact with the planet's magnetic field. We can measure these effects, and they regularly disrupt communication systems, electrical grids, and the ionosphere. But they do not only affect technology. They also coincide with shifts in human behavior.

For more than a century, researchers have observed that spikes in solar activity often align with spikes in human unrest: war, financial collapse, revolutionary movements, and mass mobilizations. In 1936, Harvard astronomer Loring B. Andrews formally documented this link after noticing that periods of high sunspot counts tracked closely with outbreaks of war, economic strain, and geopolitical tension. He suggested that fluctuations in solar radiation, particularly ultraviolet light, might subtly agitate Earth's atmosphere and, by extension, the psychological atmosphere of human societies. The idea echoed much older observations: *when the Sun is unsettled, people become unsettled.*

Solar or sunspot cycles average around 11.1 years but can range from 9.4 to 14 years. Across centuries of observation, a pattern becomes clear. High solar activity aligns with war, uprisings, disasters, and collective risk. Low solar activity often aligns with cultural output, scientific flourishing, and philosophical insight.

* * *

Recent Solar Cycle Peaks (Maximums) & Historical Correlations

SC25 — Peak ~2024–2025 (Current)

AI disruption accelerates; BRICS expansion challenges Western financial dominance; de-dollarization movements rise; Russia–Ukraine conflict escalates; Israel-Gaza war; financial system begins showing stress fractures.

SC24 — Peak ~2014

Rise of ISIS and global terror focus shifts; oil price crash destabilizes economies; Eurozone debt tensions flare; Ferguson unrest signals new civil rights era in U.S.

SC23 — Peak ~2001–2002

9/11 attacks trigger War on Terror; dot-com bubble collapses; Patriot Act launches modern surveillance state.

SC22 — Peak ~1989

Fall of the Berlin Wall signals collapse of Soviet system; Cold War order destabilizes; Exxon Valdez disaster sparks environmental awareness.

SC21 — Peak ~1979–1980

Iranian Revolution and oil shock disrupt global markets; Soviet invasion of Afghanistan begins; U.S. stagflation and crisis of confidence.

SC20 — Peak ~1968–1969

Global protest wave: Civil Rights peak, Paris '68, Prague Spring; Moon Landing marks technological triumph; Vietnam War intensifies.

SC19 — Peak ~1957–1958

Sputnik launch ignites Space Race; U.S. recession hits in 1958; nuclear arms buildup accelerates during Cold War.

SC18 — Peak ~1947–1948

Start of the Cold War; Truman Doctrine asserts U.S. global leadership; formation of Israel leads to Arab–Israeli conflicts.

SC17 — Peak ~1937–1938

Prelude to WWII: annexation of Austria and Munich Agreement; secondary crash deepens Great Depression.

SC16 — Peak ~1928

Final stock market bubble before 1929 crash; extremist politics and fascist movements gain momentum in Europe.

* * *

Scientists still debate the exact causes of sunspots, but the correlation with human excitability is well recorded. As mentioned above, climate stress does not directly cause war, but it primes societies for heightened reactivity. Solar agitation appears to act as an accelerant. Financial astrologer Christeen Skinner notes a similar tendency in the markets: during peaks in sunspot numbers, the Dow Jones index tends to rise. Collective appetite for risk increases, not only in finance but in politics, conflict, and cultural movements.

According to current data from National Aeronautics and Space Administration (NASA) and National Oceanic and Atmospheric Administration (NOAA), Solar Cycle 25 has now entered what they classify as solar maximum, but it's too early to say with certainty whether we've already passed the actual peak. What this means in practice terms is that we are in the zone of highest solar activity, or the extra spicy part of the cycle. This is the same phase that has historically lined up with spikes in conflict, technological stress, and collective agitation. According to NOAA, solar Cycle 26 is expected to begin sometime between January 2029 and December 2032.

Of note: A clear pattern emerges when the 17.7-year U.S. war rhythm is overlaid with solar cycle maxima. Most American war activation points fall within a zero to seven-year window of heightened solar activity. In other words, when the Sun enters its most geomagnetically agitated phase, the United States is almost always entering, escalating, or reorganizing around a major conflict. The closer the alignment, the more totalizing the conflict becomes.

Cycles like 1863 (Civil War), 1968–69 (Vietnam and internal revolt), and 2001–2002 (War on Terror) show near-perfect convergence between military escalation and solar maximum, and each of those moments reshaped national identity at a structural level. When the pulse of war lands just before or after a solar maximum, as in 1916–17 or 1985–86, the solar agitation coincides with buildup pressure or post-conflict reordering rather than the war peak itself.

This suggests that solar maxima do not "cause" war but they correlate with periods in which existing tensions ignite, accelerate, or become irreversible, amplifying whatever geopolitical or domestic powder keg is already in place.

* * *

Sunspots and the Economy

In 1878, British economist W. Stanley Jevons proposed a bold idea: that sunspots caused commercial crises. He argued that fluctuations in solar activity influenced weather, which in turn shaped crop yields, triggering cycles of boom and famine that rippled into business and trade. His theory built on earlier observations by Dr. Hyde Clarke, who had noted an 11-year rhythm in speculation and famine.

Decades later, in 1934, two Harvard researchers, Carlos Garcia-Mata and Felix Shaffner, set out to disprove Jevons. They expected to find no correlation between sunspots and markets. To their surprise, they discovered a strong correspondence between sunspot cycles and industrial production from 1875 to 1931. The peaks and troughs in sunspot activity lagged slightly behind those in manufacturing output, suggesting not direct causation, but a meaningful connection.

The lesson? Even if Jevons' crop theory was too simple, his instinct was probably right: solar rhythms and economic rhythms are not entirely separate.

* * *

The cycles of war, economy, and climate are not isolated events. They are expressions of a deeper pulse, a single rhythm moving through matter, markets, weather, and human emotion. Each chapter so far has traced this thread: war rising like a pressure valve, economies expanding and collapsing with new technologies, climates shifting and pushing civilizations to their breaking points.

As the Sun enters its 2024–2025 flare peak, sending charged particles across our atmosphere, it reminds us that even in an age of satellites, AI systems, and algorithmic governance, we are still responsive to forces far larger than ourselves. The oldest fire in the sky still has its way with our daily lives and civilizations.

Climate disruption intensifies resource strain. Resource strain breeds fear. Fear fractures social cohesion and turns neighbors into rivals. The Mayan collapse came after centuries of drought. The Dutch Golden Age unfolded during a mild climatic window that favored trade and innovation. The Dust Bowl brought ecological failure and economic despair in the same breath. In this light, wars are not simply political conflicts but ecological responses, triggered when systems pushed to the edge finally give way.

Solar peaks do not force us into conflict, but they turn up the voltage on whatever tension already exists. A volatile Sun paired with a stressed climate and the turnover of socioeconomic and institutional cycles creates prime conditions for small sparks to ignite into global fires.

* * *

Across the last three chapters, we traced the social cycle of generations, the war cycle, the socioeconomic cycle, climate cycles, and the solar cycle. Each moving at its own tempo, but all currently converging toward the same window in time. Generations shift their archetypal roles, wars erupt at rhythmic intervals, economies shift when their resource logic breaks down, and even the climate and sun pulse in patterns that correlate with conflict.

Each cycle explains only part of what's happening. But when looked at all together, they show that we are entering a period where many long-term patterns are all peaking at the same time:

- *Pluto ingress into Aquarius (new generation)* **2023**
- *New saeculum* **~late 2020s/early 2030s**
- *New K-wave* **~late 2020s**
- *New Socioeconomic Cycle (Friedman)* **~late 2020s**
- *Saturn-Uranus Conjunction* **2032-2035** (projected)
- *17.7-year war cycle peak* **~2020-2022** (next projected ~2039-2040)
- *53.5-year war cycle peak* **~3026-2032**
- *~100 year war cycle peak* **~2030-2050** (projected)
- *Saturn-Pluto Conjunction* **2019-2020**
- *Warm-Dry Phase (Wheeler)* **~2005-2035**
- *Solar Cycle Maximum* **~2025**

The line up of cycles turning over points to a somewhat obvious conclusion: **the 2020s and 2030s are not a random crisis period but an *on time* turning point.**

The next Cycle (2030s-2080s)

Once upon a time, power seemed to be more straightforward. Whoever controlled the land, the gold, the oil, or the biggest navy controlled the future. Resources were tangible, heavy, and obvious. But the definition of a "resource" has never been fixed. It evolves with every cycle, just like value, currency, and power itself.

For centuries, empires rose and fell on material foundations. Feudalism was built on land and agriculture. Mercantilism thrived on gold and silver. The Industrial Age ran on coal, oil, and steel. These were what armies fought over, what nations hoarded, what economies were measured by.

But the map has changed. The raw materials of empire are no longer only physical. In today's late-stage digital era, resources have become subtler, foggier, and far more psychological. The old elements—oil, minerals, land—still matter, but they've been joined, and in some cases eclipsed, by invisible currencies of the modern age.

Data, for instance, has become the new oil and is mined with every click and keystroke. Attention has become the new gold, captured by algorithms and traded by corporations. Bandwidth (both technological and mental) is a limited frontier, fought over by those who profit from our energy. Narrative control has replaced subtle propaganda; memes now move faster than missiles. And perhaps the most valuable resource of all is **trust**, a currency so scarce in a post-truth world that whole industries now exist to counterfeit it.

With all of that, physical resources are still relevant of course. In particular, the race for control of water and rare earth minerals, which are both required to physically power new technology. What oil was to the twentieth century, lithium cobalt, nickel, copper, and graphite are to the twenty-first. Without them, there are no smartphones, satellites, wind turbines, or electric cars.

The problem is that these minerals are not evenly distributed. Most are concentrated in geopolitically volatile regions: cobalt in the Congo, lithium in South America's "lithium triangle," and rare earth processing dominated by China. This uneven geography sets the stage for a global tension via a resource cold war (old story, fresh characters) because whoever controls the materials that make modern life possible, controls the pace and flavor of global power distribution.

This is the emerging battlefield of the next socioeconomic that stretches from the late 2020s/early 2030s to the 2070s/2080s. Every prior wave was defined by a foundational resource: steam and textiles (1780s–1840s), railways and coal (1840s–1890s), steel and electricity (1890s–1940s), oil and automobiles (1940s–1970s), information and telecommunications (1970s–2020s). Each began with innovation, expanded into empire, and ended in crisis.

The next cycle will likely be built on five intertwined frontiers:

- **Artificial intelligence** — the automation of cognition itself.
- **Biotechnology and synthetic biology** — reshaping life, health, and even evolution.
- **Renewable energy and rare earth minerals** — the new terrain of survival and power.
- **Space exploration** — extending the race for resources beyond Earth.
- **Consciousness technologies** — bridging the inner and outer worlds of transformation.

These aren't just new industries. They are new mythologies of power. Each represents a redefinition of what it means to create, to control, and to belong in a rapidly mutating world. As every resource revolution alters the material world, it also reshapes the systems built to govern it. The empires of the future won't rise from new materials alone, but from the institutions capable of adapting to them.

The next chapter is the political and institutional upheaval is happening right now amidst, and because of, the socioeconomic and war cycle turnover.

5

The Institutional Cycle

Cycle Length	~80-120 years
Featured Cycles	• Long Term Debt Cycle • General War Cycle • Climate Cycle • Saeculum • Uranus Cycle
Next Cycle (approx.)	Late 2020s-2110s
Key Themes of Institutional Cycle	• Multiple shorter cycles stack to force reform • Legitimacy crisis • Revolt/Restructuring • New founding mythology/solutions

The institutional cycle is a roughly 100-year rhythm in which political and administrative orders rise, stabilize, decay, and reset. We are standing at the end of one of these cycles now.

The turnover of this cycle, parallel to the turnover of all the sub-cycles from the last three chapters, is why the current institutional landscape feels as wild as it does. We are in the winter of an institutional cycle that was established immediately post WWII. All the frameworks, systems, institutions, beliefs, and expectations that were built to serve those conditions, and that cycle, are falling apart.

It's tempting to think that politics drives history. But once you start studying cycles it becomes clear that it's the other way around: politics is a reaction to cycles, not their cause. Policy is improvisation, not invention. Leaders inherit the conditions of their cycle, and their choices are shaped by the opportunities and limits of the moment.

As the institutional cycle moves into winter and the old order falters, fear, rage, and confusion rush to fill the vacuum. Institutions grow opaque, even to those running them. The U.S. federal government, once designed for wartime efficiency, has fragmented into countless agencies that rarely coordinate. To citizens, the result feels conspiratorial, as if unseen powers were orchestrating the chaos. But in truth, no one is steering the ship. The cycle itself is.

Boston, 1773.

Colonists board British ships and throw tea into the harbor in an act of direct defiance. It is no longer just resistance over taxes but a public refusal to recognize the authority of the Crown. In taverns and meeting halls, talk shifts from petitioning for rights to discussing independence outright. What had been tolerated as distant governance is now openly questioned as illegitimate.

Virginia, 1861.

The United States begins to split. State after state votes to leave the Union, and political debate gives way to armed conflict. Cannon fire at Fort Sumter marks the start of a war between former countrymen. The federal system strains as entire regions reject its authority. What follows is not just a military conflict but a forced restructuring of the nation's political foundation.

New York, 1933.

Banks close and millions lose their savings. Breadlines stretch through city streets as unemployment reaches record levels. President Roosevelt speaks over radio broadcasts, promising federal relief and a new economic direction. Confidence in both markets and government institutions is low. Overseas, authoritarian movements gain strength, signaling that the international order is entering a new phase of instability.

USA, The 2020s.

A virus shuts down schools, workplaces, and public institutions. Supply chains slow and everyday goods become uncertain. Trust in media, elections, healthcare systems, and legal authority declines sharply. At the same time, global power begins to shift as new economic blocs and financial systems rise outside traditional Western influence.

Different centuries. Different crises. But the feeling is the same.

A conviction that societies leaders, laws, and institutions aren't working. That what once felt solid has shown its hollow center. That neighbors, leaders, even entire nations have lost their minds.

This is the moment we are moving through again today. And it is right on schedule.

* * *

Institutions, like people, have lifespans. They are born in moments of necessity, grow in power, stabilize into predictability, and, when change outpaces adaptation, slowly decline into irrelevance. Eventually, they are forcibly transformed by crisis, only to be replaced by a new system.

This process is neither random nor unique to modern history. It follows a pattern, one that plays out over and over again in roughly every 80 to 120 years when the pillars of legitimacy, law, finance, and administration can no longer support the world they are meant to govern.

From the collapse of monarchies in the 18th century, to the unraveling of economic and political systems in the 1930s, to the disorientation of the early 2020s, we are reminded that stability is not the default setting of civilization. It is only one season within a larger cycle.

Institutions as Living Systems

Just as every economy rests on a foundation of resources, every society rests on a foundation of political institutions.

All the cycles we have covered are not separate events but nested gears that drive the institutional turn.

- Generational cycles, 14 to 30 years: the cast changes and with it the social mood.
- Socioeconomic cycles, 40 to 60 years: technology and markets reshape the material base.
- Debt and war cycles, 50 to 100 years: when strain peaks, resets are forced.
- Climate cycles, about 100 years: environmental stress amplifies scarcity and conflict.
- The saeculum, 80 to 120 years: the lifespan of society; mirrors its institutions

By the time an institutional order reaches maturity, it has already had to absorb two overlapping socioeconomic cycles and four or five new generations. Eventually the mismatch becomes unbearable: old institutions trying to govern new realities. The steam engine did not just move goods. It demanded new laws, new cities, new classes. Oil and the automobile did not just speed travel. They reorganized urban life and warfare. Digital networks did not just give us entertainment. They blurred borders, sovereignty, and the meaning of citizenship. Each wave pushes the order built in the last crisis toward its limits.

Institutions may resist, but they cannot outrun the pace of change.

Today, social and economic cycles are late stage, war cycles are in an active window, and climate stress is rising. The result is what the last three chapters have pointed to from different angles: a convergence zone in the 2020s and 2030s where pressure exceeds what legacy institutions can contain.

This is not the end of the world. It is the scheduled renovation built into the pattern.

The Long Waves of Debt, War, and Society

Economic cycles, as we explored in Chapter 3, sit inside the larger rhythm of institutional cycles. It often takes two ~50 year socioeconomic cycles to span one ~100 year institutional cycle. Socioeconomic cycles are driven by technology, energy, and markets while institutional cycles are political and social, shaping the architecture of power itself. Both, however, reset through crisis, or war. Debt eventually topples economic regimes. War shatters institutional ones. Together, they are the twin hard reset buttons of institutional cycles.

The Long-Term Debt Cycle

For over a century, economists and historians have noticed that capitalist economies move in long waves of roughly 50–60 years. If you remember chapter 3, you'll know these rhythms are called Kondratieff waves and are usually explained by two forces: technology and credit. We covered technology in chapter 3, but I saved the credit explanation for now. The gist is that new technologies expand access to resources. Credit determines how quickly those resources circulate. In the end, both describe the same thing: how much energy it takes to get what we need. And in the modern world, that energy is expressed through money.

At its simplest, an economy is the sum of all transactions. Every purchase is one person's spending and another's income. Credit allows us to spend money we don't yet have, betting on future income to pay it back. When credit flows freely, economies expand. When it tightens, they contract. Over short spans, this creates the familiar business cycle. Over long spans, repeated borrowing accumulates into unsustainable debt. That is when a larger reset is triggered—the long-term debt cycle.

Every other K-wave "winter" tends to be deeper and more destructive than the one before because it coincides with the culmination of the larger Long-Term Debt Cycle, long wave war cycle, and Institutional Cycle turnover.

The Long-Term Debt Cycles According to Ray Dalio

Cycle	Reserve Currency Power	Approximate Dates	Key Features	Reset Event / Transition
Dutch Guilder Cycle	Netherlands	~1600–1780	First modern financial empire; rise of central banking, credit markets, and global trade finance.	Overextension, trade wars with England, and loss of reserve currency status to Britain.
British Pound Cycle	United Kingdom	~1780–1945	Industrial Revolution, gold standard, and colonial expansion fueled by global credit dominance.	Great Depression and World War II exhausted Britain's economy; Bretton Woods (1944) shifted global leadership to the U.S.
U.S. Dollar Cycle	United States	1945–Present (projected ~2030 reset)	Dollar-based monetary order under Bretton Woods, followed by fiat money and massive debt expansion after 1971.	2008 crisis, post-2020 debt saturation, and geopolitical realignment signal a new monetary era emerging.

Dalio's research shows that each long-term debt cycle lasts roughly 75–100 years and tends to end in a systemic reset where currency regimes, power structures, and global leadership all change hands. The Dutch built the first financial empire, the British industrialized it, and the Americans digitized it.

Each rose through innovation and leverage, and each declined through overextension and debt. The current U.S. cycle is now in its late stage, when productivity stagnates, inequality widens, and money printing replaces genuine growth. According to Dalio, this is a familiar pattern that always precedes a new order.

The long-term debt cycle stretches much farther than the familiar boom-and-bust pattern we live through every decade or so. Instead of five to eight years, it unfolds over seventy-five to a hundred. Because no one lives through a full cycle, each generation mistakes its own experience for something new. But history tells the same pattern again and again: easy money, expansion, overreach, and collapse.

The Great Depression of the 1930s marked the winter phase of the last long-term debt cycle. Debt had outpaced productivity, speculation imploded, and the system broke. In 1944, the Bretton Woods Agreement rebuilt the global financial order around the U.S. dollar, launching a new cycle that carried growth through the postwar boom, the neoliberal revolution, and into our digital age.

Now, the signs of another winter are hard to miss. Debt has once again ballooned far beyond productive capacity. Inequality has hardened into structure. Central banks are running out of tools. According to Ray Dalio and others, this is what the end of a long-term debt cycle looks like. We are in a moment when old financial systems can no longer evolve, only reset.

The Bretton Woods system is ending with exhaustion for all involved. Its debt, its politics, and its promises stretched beyond repair. A new financial architecture is already forming in its place.

War Cycles

If debt resets the ledger, war resets the map. Conflict erupts when economic and technological pressures exceed what institutions can contain. As we saw in Chapter 4, war follows its own nested rhythms: small flare-ups around every 8.8 years, mobilization peaks every 17.7, and larger geopolitical alignments around every 53.5 years. These longer arcs, which Raymond Wheeler and Edward Dewey identified as "general wars," tend to coincide with major financial collapses and political restructuring—otherwise known as the institutional cycle.

War Cycles

Cycle Type	Duration	Composition	Typical Characteristics	Historical Examples
Minor War Cycle	~8.8 years	—	Local or limited conflicts, proxy wars, regional tensions. Often preludes or aftermaths of larger wars.	-1991 Gulf War -1999 Kosovo -2008 Georgia -2016–24 proxy wars (Ukraine, Middle East)
War Cycle	~17.7 years	Two 8.8-year cycles	Periods of heightened global tension or mid-scale war activity.	-1776–1793 (Revolution) -1914–1931 (WWI aftermath → rise of fascism) -2001–2018 (9/11 → GWOT).
Major War Cycle	~53 years	Three 17.7-year cycles	"Systemic wars" that reshape empires, borders, and power structures.	-1850s Crimean War -1900s–1940s World Wars -1950s–2000s Cold War / Terror era -2020s emerging multipolar conflicts
General War Cycle	~100–106 years	Two 53-year cycles	Civilization-scale resets involving both economic and institutional collapse and reorganization.	-1618–1648 Thirty Years War -1790s–1815 Napoleonic Era -1914-1945 World Wars I & II -2030s–2050s = next inflection

Layered beneath these human cycles are the climate phases Wheeler mapped: Cold-Dry periods of austerity, Warm-Wet expansions, Warm-Dry peaks of authoritarianism and external war, and Cold-Wet cycles of internal revolt and democratic restructuring. We are currently in a Warm-Dry phase (2005–2035), which Wheeler consistently found to be the highest-risk window for systemic conflict, especially when paired with K-wave crests and debt cycle exhaustion.

Debt peaks compress political options. Societies caught between obligation and survival can no longer paper over contradictions. Distributional fights intensify. Consensus collapses. War—whether fought through soldiers, data, sanctions, or currency—becomes the blunt instrument of reorganization. It redistributes claims, resets hierarchies, and establishes new myths of legitimacy.

This is why debt supercycles, climate stress peaks, and war crests so often arrive together. They are synchronized corrections that force equilibrium back into human systems. Each time, the world emerges reordered: new currencies, new alliances, new ideologies, new maps. Marx called wars the "express trains of history." If that is true, we can already hear the whistle.

The Saeculum

Every new institutional cycle is born with a promise and an organizing story that feels fresh and true to the people who lived through its founding crisis. Institutions are created to solve the problems of the previous cycle's winter. But over time, problems change. What once felt visionary hardens into bureaucracy. Rules multiply. Cynicism creeps in. The system that once solved problems begins to create them.

In chapter 3 we discussed how generations, marked by Pluto's transit, are the heartbeat of social change. Every 4-6 (depending on where Pluto is in its orbit) generations combine to create a saeculum, or a long human life. When we apply the saeculum concept to political institutions instead of people we get the institutional cycle. Going back to Strauss and Howe's fourth turning framework, we can see how each turning ushers in a new generational archetype with its own mood and orientation toward power:

- Spring (Prophets) build the vision after crisis.
- Summer (Nomads) consolidate and defend it.
- Fall (Heroes) challenge and reform it.
- Winter (Artists) dissolve what no longer works and seed what comes next.

When the fourth generation reaches maturity, institutions that once felt permanent have become hollow shells of their original intent. That's when the saecular "winter," or the Fourth Turning, arrives, demanding renewal through upheaval.

Seen this way, the *saeculum* is not just a demographic curiosity. It's the inner rhythm of the institutional cycle itself.. It explains why bureaucracies lose moral vitality after about a century, why revolutions tend to skip a few generations, and why societies forget the lessons that once defined them.

Each *saeculum* ends when memory runs out. And that's precisely where we are now: the institutions built in the wake of World War II, such as the Bretton Woods order, the UN, NATO, the American constitutional consensus, have reached the end of their generational lifespan. The founders are gone and a new generation is inheriting the task of reinvention.

* * *

Winters Aren't New

One of the reasons I love history is because it gives a good old fashioned perspective check (which many of us need right now). Whatever you're feeling — the fear, the outrage, the exhaustion, or even the sense of victory or progress — none of it is as unique as it feels. We are not the first generation to wrestle with winter, and we are not the first to fight for something new.

Every saeculum ends in Winter, and every Winter feels like the end of the world while you're living through it. But in hindsight, each is simply another season of the same rhythm — bringing both devastation and renewal. Right now, as we love to look around and love to play the world's smallest violin for ourselves, I find it helpful to look at previous winter seasons and their corresponding spring:

Approximate years	*Crisis / Collapse*	*Renewal / Breakthrough*
1773–1794	*French & American Revolutions topple monarchies and empires. Violence, guillotines, wars.*	*Birth of constitutions, democracy, and the modern idea of rights and legitimacy.*
1854-1877	*American Civil War splits the republic; 750,000 dead; nation nearly dissolves.*	*Abolition of slavery; a constitutional rebirth around freedom and union.*
1929–1946	*Great Depression and World War II devastate economies; tens of millions killed.*	*Rise of the UN, GI Bill, civil rights momentum, and a global order that sustained (imperfect) peace for decades.*
2001-late 2020s/early 2030s	*COVID-19 pandemic, political violence, institutional rot, financial shocks, global fragmentation.*	*Breakthroughs in medicine, digital technology, and new forms of solidarity and global awareness beginning to emerge.*

We are not special in our defeats, and we are not special in our victories. We are simply the ones living through this Winter, which will eventually turn into Spring. And I don't know about you but I'd still take this Winter over living through the trenches of Verdun or the guillotine in Paris.

* * *

To further illustrate the American saeculum, let's go back to Strauss and Howe's turning framework. From the founding generation onward, America has moved through four saeculums, each ending in a Crisis that reshaped the republic and gave birth to a new order.

The Revolutionary Saeculum (1704–1794)

- **High (1704–1727):** Colonial expansion, strong local communities.
- **Awakening (1727–1746):** The First Great Awakening (religious revival).
- **Unraveling (1746–1773):** Fracturing with Britain, distrust of monar-

chy.
- **Crisis (1773–1794):** *American Revolution* (1775–1783), U.S. Constitution (1787–1789).

The Civil War Saeculum (1794–1865)

- **High (1794–1822):** Early Republic, Era of Good Feelings, expansion, confidence
- **Awakening (1822–1844):** The Second Great Awakening, reform movements, abolitionism, religious revivals
- **Unraveling (1844–1854):** Mexican–American War, Compromise of 1850, intensifying sectional conflict. Trust erodes, polarization hardens.
- **Crisis (1860–1865):** "Bleeding Kansas," *Civil War*, Reconstruction, Second Republic

The Great Power Saeculum (1865–1946)

- **High (1877-1901):** Reconstruction, Gilded Age, rise of industrial capitalism, railroads, monopolies, mass immigration
- **Awakening (1901-1924):** Progressive Era, labor movements, suffragism, prohibition
- **Unraveling (1924–1929):** Roaring Twenties, rising cultural individualism, disillusionment with WWI, Crash of 1929
- **Crisis (1929–1946):** *Great Depression* (1929–1939), *World War II* (1939–1945). Global authoritarian threat. Birth of modern state and new global hegemony

The Millennial Saeculum (1946–late 2020s/early 2030s)

- **High (1946–1964):** Post-WWII boom, suburban growth, Cold War order.
- **Awakening (1964–1984):** Counterculture, Civil Rights, feminism, spiritual ferment.

- **Unraveling (1984–2001):** Deregulation, privatization, culture wars, institutional decline.
- **Crisis (2001–?):** 9/11, *Global War on Terror* (2001-2021), 2008 crash, COVID-19 pandemic, political and social fragmentation

Across 250 years, the American story has followed the saecular rhythm with startling fidelity: strong institutions → cultural awakening → unraveling → crisis and renewal. Each Crisis felt unprecedented, each reordered the system, and each cleared space for a new institutional order to emerge.

Geopolitical strategist George Friedman describes a nearly identical rhythm in American institutions. In his framing, the United States has passed through three great cycles so far, each lasting about 80 years:

- **The Founding Cycle (1787–1865):** From the Constitution to the Civil War, when unresolved tensions finally tore the system apart.
- **The Industrial Cycle (1865–1945):** From Reconstruction through industrial expansion, culminating in the Depression and World War II.
- **The Technocratic Cycle (1945–2025?):** The era of expertise, bureaucracy, and centralized authority now faltering under polarization, distrust, and institutional breakdown.

While Friedman essentially starts his count at the beginning of the Civil War saeculum, he also concludes that we are currently at the edge of systemic reinvention. America is not collapsing; it is shifting between institutional cycles, just as it has before. This is not the fault of any party, person, religious group, race, gender, ideology, or technology. We are in the deep Winter of the Millennial Saeculum, a Crisis phase that will run its course before settling into a new American order.

And if both historians and strategists can trace the same rhythm in America's past, the resonance grows even stronger when we turn to the sky.

Uranus and the American Saeculum

If history can reveal a rhythm to America's institutional life, planetary influence adds another dimension that shows us the deeper archetypal energies at play (back to that cosmic clock). In the case of the Institutional cycle, the cosmic timekeeper is Uranus.

Every 84 years, Uranus completes a full orbit around the Sun and returns to where it began, delivering a collective jolt of awakening. That's roughly the span of a long human life, a saeculum, and an institutional cycle.

On the personal level, Uranus transit through an individual's birth chart brings the same energy of liberation. Around age forty-two (the Uranus opposition) people face the so-called midlife awakening, when the soul pushes to break free from roles that no longer fit. On the societal scale, that opposition comes halfway through each saeculum, at at the point of the socioeconomic cycle turnover, stirring rebellion and cultural realignment. By the time Uranus returns to where it started, roughly 84 years later, a civilization has shed its skin entirely and stepped into a new era.

In astrology, Uranus rules electricity, revolution, invention, and all things that accelerate human progress. It governs the collective nervous system and our capacity to think faster, connect farther, and break free from what feels outdated. In mundane terms, it symbolizes technology, science, railways, aviation, communication, and the human drive for freedom. Uranus symbolizes *the people's power*: from parliaments and assemblies to strikes and rebellions.

Uranus has been transiting Taurus for the last 7 years (2018–2025), a phase marked by disruption in money, land, agriculture, food systems, and our relationship to stability and work. Cryptocurrency, inflation shocks, and food supply anxiety all echo this signature. When Uranus entered Gemini on July 8, 2025 (where it will stay until May 22, 2033), the energy of change accelerates. What began in Taurus as a shake-up of resources and values now moves into information, language, and perception. Gemini is mutable air, meaning it is fast, dual, curious, and unstable. Uranus feels right at home in this element. Expect rapid transformations in how we think, communicate, travel, and trade. The world will feel like it's moving at double speed. Ideas will spread (and polarize) at lightning pace.

Attention becomes currency even more than it already is. The battlefield shifts from land to mind. Expect a wave of innovation in AI, quantum computing, neural interfaces, and immersive communication technologies. But with every breakthrough comes instability and in Gemini this looks like misinformation, propaganda wars, algorithmic control, and the disintegration of shared truth.

Historically, Uranus in Gemini coincides with periods of mental, technological, and political revolution. Often this includes literal wars of ideas or of "brothers." Gemini, after all, is the archetype of duality, or two sides of the same coin. This has manifested as America fighting for its independence from big brother Britain, the US civil war, ideological conflicts, and identity crises within nations. America's last two Uranus-in-Gemini periods both involved wars of self-definition: the Revolutionary War, the Civil War, and World War II where America emerged as a world superpower.

Under this transit, opposites tend to polarize and mirror each other, forcing societies to confront their ideological doubles. Civil wars, revolts, and revolutions against established powers are common, but so are breathtaking leaps in human ingenuity.

Years	Historical Precedent of Uranus in Gemini
1775–1782	*The American Revolution*: radical ideas of liberty spread through pamphlets like Paine's *Common Sense*. Humanity takes flight with the first hot air balloons.
1859–1866	*The Telegraph Era*: the first transatlantic cable connects continents; communication transforms war strategy during the U.S. Civil War. Neptune in Aries at the same time fuels ideological fervor.
1941–1949	*World War II and the Information Age*: radar, jet engines, codebreaking, nuclear power, and the birth of computers reshape reality. Propaganda and mass media become weapons of war and influence.

With Pluto simultaneously in Aquarius, the two archetypes of revolution and reinvention work together to dismantle centralized power and birth new, decentralized systems. We will likely see peer-to-peer economies, community power grids, alternative education, and fluid social structures no longer bound to the old hierarchies. As the U.S. approaches its next Uranus return, the struggle may unfold not through territory but through information: what we believe, how we know, and whom we trust. (*For more on the Uranus transit see chapter seven*).

Another possible manifestation of this transit also aligning with the war cycle is the evolution of warfare from 4th to 5th generation. Fourth-generation warfare dissolved the boundaries between state and non-state actors. Fifth-generation warfare dissolves the boundary between war and daily life. Under this model, victory is not achieved by capturing territory but by capturing attention, belief, and narrative authority.

Fifth-generation warfare is not about who has the most tanks. It is about who can fracture trust, disrupt cohesion, and weaponize interdependence. Its tactics might include:

- **Cyberwarfare**: disabling infrastructure, hacking systems, targeting communication.
- **Economic warfare**: sanctions, supply chain disruptions, and weaponized debt.
- **Narrative warfare**: propaganda campaigns, deep-fakes, disinformation, and meme-driven influence operations.

- **Social warfare**: algorithmic amplification of division, identity fragmentation, the engineering of internal conflict.

In this model, war looks less like Normandy and more like destabilized elections, collapsing supply chains, manipulated identities, and psychic exhaustion. It is invasive but often invisible, not marked by explosions but by fractures in the collective fabric.

* * *

Here's the bottom line: **institutions aren't forever.** They're built in one moment of history, stretched to manage the next, and eventually pushed past their breaking point. What is considered a valuable resource changes as technologies leap forward. Debt cycles show us that money math eventually becomes political. The fight over who pays, who benefits, who gets squeezed eventually spills into the culture. War cycles remind us that when those tensions can't the human lifetime rhythm where each generation builds, questions, unravels, and finally breaks the system they've inherited, and you've got a recipe for regular institutional overhaul.

Think of these cycles not as separate events, but as nested gears, each turning the next:

- **Generational cycles (14–30 years)** introduce new psychological archetypes — the cast changes.
- **Socioeconomic cycles (40–60 years)** strain the material base — the economy shifts underfoot.
- **Debt and war cycles (50–100 years)** act as pressure valves — when strain peaks, the system forces a reset.
- **Climate cycles (around 100 years)** add environmental stress, amplifying conflict and scarcity.

- **Saeculum (80–120 years)** measure the lifespan of the social order itself — mirroring the arc of the institutions that society built from rise to decay to rebirth.

All of these rhythms build toward an institutional reset that happens once every 80 to 120 years, when old structures can no longer solve modern problems and new institutions are required. What feels unprecedented now is simply unfamiliar. History has passed through the turning of this cycle many times, and now it is our turn.

In the next chapter, we widen the lens beyond institutions (and the span of a human lifetime) to the 500 year global cycle: the long arc of empire, hegemony, and civilizational transformation.

6

The Global Cycle

Cycle Length	~500 years
Featured Cycles	<ul><li>World System Theory</li><li>Pluto Return</li><li>Human Design Global Programming Cycle</li><li>Wheeler's Drought Cycle</li><li>Neptune-Pluto Cycle</li></ul>
Next Cycle (approx.)	~2020s-2500s
Key Themes of Global Cycle	<ul><li>Reorganization of global power</li><li>Mass migrations</li><li>New ways of organizing people, power, resources</li><li>New collective identity/myths</li></ul>

In the last chapter, we tracked how institutions rise and fall on roughly 80–120 year rhythms. They're born out of crisis, grow strong, then calcify until they no longer match the world they were built for. Eventually, they collapse under the weight of debt, war, and generational turnover.

But institutions don't live in isolation. They sit inside a larger container: the global system itself.

And when that container shifts, no institution can escape.

The global system we've lived in for the past five centuries is the marriage of capitalism and the nation-state. It emerged from the wreckage of feudalism, was shaped in the crucible of empire and industrialization, and has given us the modern world as we know it. For centuries, it looked invincible as it delivered order, growth, and legitimacy. But like any system, it has a lifespan.

Just as the medieval Church once lost its monopoly on legitimacy, the nation-state is losing its grip. Its tools—currency monopoly, taxation, national identity—are being eroded by digital technologies, ecological strain, demographic collapse, and ideological exhaustion. Governments are doubling down with more control—surveillance, censorship, nationalism— but these aren't signs of strength. They're the spasms of a system past its prime.

This isn't just another financial downturn or political squabble. It's the end of a 500-year global cycle. Feudalism once unraveled into capitalism and nation-states. Now capitalism and the nation-state are shifting into something new.

At this point the information will intentionally be shorter and unintention- ally be more vague. Talking about a 500-year cycle is where most people's eyes begin to glaze over, since it feels so out of reach. But it is important to talk about for two reasons. The first is that it is turning over right now. So all of the more immediate, tactical shifts that are happening with the shorter cycles are happening against the backdrop of this large, long, slow moving cycle. It's like jogging on solid ground versus jogging on a moving walkway. Everything feels extra...accelerated.

Let's get into it.

The 500-Year World System

World-systems theory gives us a wider frame for understanding where we are right now. If Chapter 5 showed that institutions have lifespans of 80–120 years, world-systems last 400 to 500 years. They're the containers inside which institutions rise and fall multiple times. Nested cycles within nested cycles.

The world system we're living in today was born from the late Middle Ages. Feudalism had exhausted itself: land-based wealth couldn't keep up with growing trade, technology, and population. Out of its fall came new forces: merchants, markets, banking, and the rise of territorial states able to tax and wage war. By the 1500s, Europe had birthed a new world-system, one that spread outward through empire and colonization until it set the terms of global order.

Historians like Fernand Braudel and Immanuel Wallerstein mapped this shift with precision. They showed that capitalism was never just an economy but a way of organizing the entire world, structuring power, and creating legitimacy and meaning. The nation-state provided the political structure, while capitalism provided the economic logic. Together, they became the operating system of modern civilization.

But, like economies, societies, and institutions, world-systems aren't eternal. They have beginnings, middles, and ends. Roman Imperialism had one. Feudalism had one. And capitalism + the nation-state had its time in the sun. However, the signs of a system at the end of its cycle are becoming evident: debt overload, ecological overshoot, demographic decline, legitimacy crises.

For Wallerstein, the end of a world-system isn't neat or linear. As an entity in and of itself, the world system enters what he called a period of "wild oscillations," or a drawn-out transition where the old structures lose legitimacy, new prototypes emerge, and the system lurches between competing futures. These oscillations can last for decades. They look and feel chaotic because they are (hence where we are right now). The fourth or fifth Institutional cycle is at an end, financial systems swing widely between inflation and deflation, empires overextend and retract, and people lose faith in the ideologies that once made sense of the world. Everyone knows the old system no longer works, but no one can fully articulate the new one. (Seriously. Imagine explaining daily life in 2025 to someone in 1525.)

The last world system, or global cycle, turnover was in the late Middle Ages. As feudalism was breaking down, Europe swung through waves of famine, plague, peasant revolts, religious schisms, and endless wars. Yet in the middle of that turbulence, merchants, bankers, and new forms of statecraft were taking root—laying the groundwork for capitalism and the nation-state to eventually stabilize as the new order. That's exactly the kind of liminal space we're in today. The nation-state and capitalism are fraying, prototypes of new systems are everywhere, and the world is oscillating wildly between breakdown and experimentation.

The Nation-State as the Container (and Why It's Shifting)

The nation-state has been the central container of the modern world-system for nearly 400 years. The idea of the nation-state was born in 1648 with the Peace of Westphalia, matured through 18th–19th century nationalism, and became globally institutionalized after World War II (1945).

But it wasn't inevitable— it was invented to solve the problems of a certain time and place. In the wake of feudalism's increasing failures, early modern rulers in Europe needed new ways to organize power, wage wars, and finance expansion. They couldn't rely on local lords or the Church anymore; they needed broader, more centralized forms of legitimacy.

Enter the earliest concepts of the nation-state, before it was known as such. From the 1500s onward, monarchs began consolidating territories into unified realms with centralized taxation, standing armies, and standardized laws. But armies and taxes alone don't hold people together. What bound these new political units was the invention of *national identity*. For the first time, people were told that they belonged not just to a village or a lord, but to a larger imagined community.

Take the French Revolution as an example. When the monarchy fell, the revolutionaries didn't just replace a king with another ruler, they invented the idea of the *citizen*. Suddenly, to be French wasn't just to live under a crown; it was to be part of a collective people, equal under the law, bound by shared symbols like the tricolor flag, the Marseillaise anthem, and a story of common destiny. That national identity made it possible to mobilize mass armies and sustain a modern state.

The same process played out later in the 19th century with German and Italian unification. Dozens of fragmented states and duchies were stitched together into "Germany" and "Italy," not just by force, but by cultivating myths of common language, heritage, and culture. These weren't timeless identities but intentionally crafted, often from above, to rally people behind a new political order.

Nationalism was revolutionary. It made it possible to mobilize entire populations for industrial wars, to justify taxation as a shared civic duty, and to tie personal prosperity to the fate of the state. In short, the nation-state became the mythology that made capitalism work.

For centuries, this arrangement looked unshakable. But every container eventually outlives the conditions that gave it strength. Today, the nation-state is faltering under pressures it was never designed to manage. Capital flows freely across borders in ways taxation can't keep up with. Digital technologies undermine the idea of centralized currency and even centralized identity. Demographic decline erodes the military and tax base. And ecological limits expose how fragile growth-based legitimacy really is.

In a globalized, digitized world, the old promise that your identity and future are bound up with a single nation is becoming less helpful or necessary. The European Union tried to create a supranational identity, but most people never fully bought into "being European" the way they did "being French" or "being German." At the same time, people have begun retreating into smaller, more personal forms of identity: regions, ethnic groups, religious movements, even digital tribes and online communities. The gravitational pull is no longer toward bigger national entities, but toward tighter, more resonant ones.

The result is a legitimacy crisis. Nation-states still wield armies and borders, but they no longer inspire the same loyalty they once did. Just as the medieval Church lost its monopoly on legitimacy, the nation-state is slowly losing its grip. Its ability to serve as the primary vessel for human identity and economic life is breaking down and we the people know it. The response of most governments has been to double down on control with more surveillance, more censorship, more border restrictions, more authoritarian posturing. However, this is only a phase before a new world system coalesces in the next century or so.

Ideologies in Flux

Every world-system carries its own set of legitimizing ideologies, or mythology. Stories that make its institutions feel natural and inevitable. Speaking very broadly for the modern American system, those ideologies were primarily democracy, capitalism, and, for a time, communism as its rival. Each fit the needs of the nation-state era. Democracy promised representation within the boundaries of a state. Capitalism promised growth that could be distributed through national markets. Communism offered an alternative myth of solidarity, tied to the same industrial logic.

For a while, these stories worked. They gave people a sense that their personal lives were bound to the success of their nation, that prosperity and stability were possible if they played by the rules. But today, those rules no longer line up with reality. Democracy feels hollow when corporate money shapes elections and digital media erodes public trust. Capitalism is sputtering under ecological limits, inequality, and burnout. Communism as a state project largely collapsed decades ago, but the broader socialist tradition has never gone away and is currently supported by younger generations in the U.S. and Europe questioning neoliberal capitalism.

But at the end of the day, people are starting to see through the 'isms' that have defined us—questioning whether they can actually follow through on their promises.

When old ideologies lose their grip, people start searching for new ones. And now, instead of rallying around grand narratives like "the nation" or "capitalism," people are experimenting with smaller, more local, and more personal stories. Some are turning toward spirituality and wellness. Others toward online movements, niche communities, or alternative economies. Digital tribes, lifestyle ideologies, and micro-identities are filling the vacuum left by national myths and expired promises.

Geopolitical Reordering

For the past three decades, we've lived in what scholars call a *unipolar moment*: a world dominated by the United States after the Cold War. For a brief moment, it seemed like this order could last indefinitely. The U.S. military was unmatched, global trade ran on American security guarantees, and the dollar was the unquestioned reserve currency. But, as you know now from getting this far into the book, nothing lasts forever.

Today, that dominance is slipping. The U.S. remains powerful but stretched thin and increasingly unwilling to underwrite globalization. Meanwhile, new regional powers are rising not necessarily to replace America as a global hegemon, but to assert control over their neighborhoods. Turkey is flexing in the Middle East, Japan is rearming, Poland is positioning as Europe's eastern anchor. China and Russia loom large in headlines, but both carry serious long-term weaknesses. For instance, China faces demographic collapse and economic fragility while Russia is burning resources in Ukraine.

Geopolitical strategist Peter Zeihan argues that the era of seamless globalization is over. Without U.S. naval power securing sea lanes, global supply chains will fragment. Trade will shrink. Regions will become more self-contained and competitive. Whether or not you agree with all of Zeihan's forecasts, his basic point is aligned to the season: the global order built after 1945 is unraveling.

What comes next is not another clean handoff from one hegemon to another, but something messier: multipolarity. Instead of one global center of gravity, power will be distributed across regions, each with its own security arrangements, currencies, and spheres of influence. This fits the broader cycle: just as institutions and ideologies are fragmenting into smaller, more local identities, so too is geopolitics.

Crisis of Capitalism

Now for the topic everyone loves to hate: capitalism. For five centuries, it has powered expansion, innovation, and growth. But capitalism was never just an economic system. It has been a worldview. Growth wasn't just a policy but meaning, purpose, and power itself. Nations, states, towns, and families justified their existence by constantly pushing for *more*: more production, more consumption, more GDP.

That logic worked as long as there were frontiers to exploit, resources to tap, and populations to grow into new markets. But now? Inequality has exploded, hollowing out the middle classes that capitalism once relied on. Ecological systems are straining under relentless extraction and carbon buildup. Workers are burning out in economies that demand endless productivity while offering less stability. In short: capitalism has run into the limits of its own success.

This isn't just an economic problem. It's a legitimacy problem. People can feel that the deal has changed. The promise that hard work and participation in the system will deliver prosperity is very clearly a scam. For younger generations, home ownership, stable jobs, and retirement security are out of reach. For many in the world, integration into global capitalism has meant volatility and dependency more than shared prosperity.

In past eras, crises of legitimacy pushed societies to adopt new orders. The feudal system ended not just because of plagues and revolts, but because it could no longer explain or deliver on people's needs. Capitalism is in that position now. It still dominates, but its story is not working the way that it used to. The cracks are visible in everything from housing protests to ecological movements, from the rise of "anti-work" culture to decentralized finance.

Like institutions and nation-states, capitalism will not disappear overnight. It may even persist, but it will be in a different form.

Energetic & Mythic Shifts

So far, we've looked at the structural breakdown: institutions, nation-states, ideologies, geopolitics, capitalism. But before systems collapse or change materially, they must shift energetically and symbolically first.

America's Pluto Return (2022-2024)

It was a humid summer in Philadelphia, 1776. Inside the Pennsylvania State House, delegates debated rebellion. Signing the Declaration of Independence would brand them traitors to the British Crown. If they failed, they would hang. But they did it anyway.

What those revolutionaries couldn't have known was that their defiance coincided with a deeper rhythm of time. In 1776, Pluto—the planet of death, power, and transformation—stood at 27° Capricorn. Two and a half centuries later, between 2022 and 2024, Pluto returned to that exact position.

A Pluto Return occurs once every 248 years, far longer than a human lifetime but close to the lifespan of nations and empires. It marks a collective reckoning: the death of one order and the birth of another. When Pluto returns to its natal point, everything built under its original influence comes under review.

For the United States, Pluto in Capricorn governs power, systems, and institutions like governments, banks, militaries, and hierarchies of control. The nation was *born* during Pluto in Capricorn, so its karmic DNA is tied to building and maintaining power structures.

We can look to other empires Pluto returns to see the same rhythm. Rome's first Pluto Return (264 BCE) marked its transformation from an Italian republic to a Mediterranean power through the Punic Wars. By its second Return (218 CE), the empire was fracturing under economic strain, civil war, and plague. Britain's Pluto Return (1940–1952) coincided with the de facto end of the British Empire and the rise of American dominance. Pluto brings empires to maturity. It is up to them whether they rise to the occasion of another round and slowly fade away.

Now, as Pluto has just finished its time in Capricorn and entered Aquarius

(2023–2043), that process is shifting from the material to the digital. Power is moving away from centralized hierarchies toward distributed networks like blockchains, decentralized finance, AI systems, and new global alignments. The United States, founded as the prototype of the modern state, is now confronting the limits of that model. Its institutions were built for an industrial, territorial world, meaning that there is a lot of change that needs to happen in order to govern a post-industrial, digital one.

As we discussed in chapter two, Pluto doesn't destroy for destruction's sake. It exposes what has rotted and demands transformation. The U.S. is being forced to confront corruption, inequality, and overreach within the same frameworks it once exported to the world: finance, democracy, and military power. The pressure we feel through political polarization, institutional distrust, and economic instability to name a few, is the natural consequence of resisting that reform.

If America evolves, this Pluto Return could become facilitate a "glow up" rather than a fall. It offers a chance to decentralize power, modernize democracy, and lead through innovation rather than dominance. If it doesn't, the weight of the old system will keep collapsing under its own contradictions.

Pluto Transit	Dates	Historical Expression
Pluto at 27° Capricorn	1776-1777	Declaration of Independence signed; Articles of Confederation drafted
Pluto square U.S. Pluto	1848–1850	Sectional crisis, expansion debates, lead-up to Civil War.
Pluto opposite U.S. Pluto	1936–1939	Great Depression, rise of fascism, birth of New Deal order.
Pluto Return to 27° Capricorn	2022–2024	Institutional decay, populist polarization, digital power revolution.

Pluto's message is simple but unforgiving: evolve or decay. Rome faced it. Britain faced it. Now it's America's turn.

Human Design and Global Programming Cycles

All the themes we have stressed so far—decentralization, sovereignty, etc.—line up beautifully with another esoteric tool called Human Design. The Human Design system is a holistic map of consciousness, combining elements of astrology, the I Ching, Kabbalah, and Vedic philosophy. It was channeled by Alan Robert Krakower (Ra Uru Hu) after a mystical experience in 1987 and published in *The Human Design System* (1992). At its core, Human Design explores the mechanics of auras, or the way individual energy fields interact, make decisions, and move through life. Each person's "bodygraph" functions like a blueprint, showing how energy is designed to flow through them.

While most people engage with Human Design for personal growth, the system also describes global programming cycles. These are four-hundred-year background frequencies that shape collective consciousness. These cycles function like the incarnation crosses that define individual lives, but on a planetary scale. Just as an individual incarnation cross sets the theme of a lifetime, each global cycle sets the energetic atmosphere for all of humanity.

According to Human Design, these cycles are influenced by the continuous stream of neutrinos, or subatomic particles emitted by stars (especially the sun), that pass through our bodies at all times. Though tiny, neutrinos carry mass and information. Human Design teaches that these particles imprint us with cosmic coding, essentially "programming" both individuals and the collective field. Every cycle brings a new neutrino backdrop, naturally shifting the patterns of human thought, behavior, and social organization.

The Cross of Planning (1615–2027) defined the era we are leaving. Its themes revolved around tribe, systems, and external authority:

- Sacrificing the self for the "good of the tribe" (family, nation, corporation).

- Building massive institutions: banks, universities, militaries, governments, hospitals.
- Logic, science, and reason as guiding frameworks.
- Collective reliance on external cues (jobs, religions, laws) to direct life energy.
- A masculine-coded model of power: push, force, initiate.

The shadow side of this cycle (now glaringly visible) has been our collective over-dependence on institutions. For generations, we treated them like parental figures: benevolent, all-knowing, responsible for our safety. We were conditioned to believe that obedience made us "good" and that survival depended on staying inside the lines they drew. Faith in governments, corporations, and systems created both stability and deep codependency. As the global incarnation cross changes, we are becoming more aware of this patterning and rebelling against it.

The incoming paradigm, **The Cross of the Sleeping Phoenix (2027–2438)** ushers in a radically different era, sometimes called the era of the individual. Its themes include:

- Differentiation. Meaning no more one-size-fits-all solutions.
- Self-reliance and sovereignty: heal yourself, support yourself, find your own truth.
- New (old) ways of work and survival: side hustles, off-grid living, homeschooling, peer-to-peer networks.
- Personal responsibility: put on your own oxygen mask first, then help the tribe.
- Feminine-coded power: responsive, patient, collaborative, embodied.

This shift does not mean people will stop caring for one another. It means we will no longer abandon ourselves in service to institutions or abstract collective ideals. The health of the whole will be recognized as inseparable from the integrity of the individual. For centuries people have traded their personal truth for safety, and it has produced generations of bitter people living out quietly resentful lives. With this new incarnation cross, that illusion of safety is dissolving. Without it, we are left with both the opportunity and the responsibility to follow the path that is uniquely ours. And in doing so, we are actually serving the collective in a truer way.

Under the old paradigm, this would have been dismissed as selfish. In reality, it mirrors a core teaching in Kabbalah: every soul carries a specific fragment of creation to repair, or a spark of intention that only it can bring into form. When we follow our true desire, not the one shaped by fear or approval but the one that rises from this essence, we are not acting in self-interest. We are fulfilling our role in the larger design. The old world equated goodness with obedience and uniformity. The new world recognizes that *alignment is service*. When each person lives from their true design, the result is not disorder. It is coherence, like a symphony finally allowing every instrument to play its rightful part.

As the neutrino streams shift us into this new backdrop, we should expect continued breakdown of the old ways: loss of faith in government, banking, medicine, academia, and hierarchical religion. The Cross of the Sleeping Phoenix asks us to embody sovereignty, self-expression, and personal coherence as the building blocks of a new collective.

Global Cycles - The Global Consciousness Program
From: 16,513 BC - 3,674 AD

Period						Cross					Cross
16513-16102 BC	The Lock	1	2	7	13	Cross of the Sphinx	46	25	15	10	Cross of the Vessel of Love
16101-15688 BC	The Key	44	24	33	19	Cross of the Four Ways	6	36	12	11	Cross of Eden
15689-15278 BC	The Key	28	27	31	41	Cross of the Unexpected	47	22	45	26	Cross of Rulership
15277-14866 BC	The Key	50	3	56	60	Cross of Laws	64	63	35	5	Cross of Consciousness
14865-14454 BC	The Key	32	42	62	61	Cross of Maya	40	37	16	9	Cross of Planning
14453-14042 BC	The Key	57	51	53	54	Cross of Penetration	59	55	20	34	Cross of the Sleeping Phoenix
14041-13630 BC	The Key	48	21	39	38	Cross of Tension	29	30	8	14	Cross of Contagion
13629-13218 BC	The Key	18	17	62	58	Cross of Service	4	49	23	43	Cross of Explanation
13217-12806 BC	The Lock	46	25	15	10	Cross of the Vessel of Love	7	13	2	1	Cross of the Sphinx
12805-12394 BC	The Key	6	36	12	11	Cross of Eden	33	19	24	44	Cross of the Four Ways
12393-11982 BC	The Key	47	22	45	26	Cross of Rulership	31	41	27	28	Cross of the Unexpected
11981-11570 BC	The Key	64	63	35	5	Cross of Consciousness	56	60	3	50	Cross of Laws
11569-11158 BC	The Key	40	37	16	9	Cross of Planning	62	61	42	32	Cross of Maya
11157-10746 BC	The Key	59	55	20	34	Cross of the Sleeping Phoenix	53	54	51	57	Cross of Penetration
10745-10334 BC	The Key	29	30	8	14	Cross of Contagion	39	38	21	48	Cross of Tension
10333-9922 BC	The Key	4	49	23	43	Cross of Explanation	52	58	17	18	Cross of Service
9921-9510 BC	The Lock	7	13	2	1	Cross of the Sphinx	15	10	25	46	Cross of the Vessel of Love
9509-9098 BC	The Key	33	19	24	44	Cross of the Four Ways	12	11	36	6	Cross of Eden
9097-8686 BC	The Key	31	41	27	28	Cross of the Unexpected	45	26	22	47	Cross of Rulership
8685-8274 BC	The Key	56	60	3	50	Cross of Laws	35	5	63	64	Cross of Consciousness
8273-7862 BC	The Key	62	61	42	32	Cross of Maya	16	9	37	40	Cross of Planning
7861-7450 BC	The Key	53	54	51	57	Cross of Penetration	20	34	65	59	Cross of the Sleeping Phoenix
7449-7038 BC	The Key	39	38	21	48	Cross of Tension	8	14	30	29	Cross of Contagion
7037-6626 BC	The Key	52	58	17	18	Cross of Service	23	43	49	4	Cross of Explanation
6625-6214 BC	The Lock	15	10	25	46	Cross of the Vessel of Love	2	1	13	7	Cross of the Sphinx
6213-5802 BC	The Key	12	11	36	6	Cross of Eden	24	44	19	33	Cross of the Four Ways
5801-5390 BC	The Key	46	26	22	47	Cross of Rulership	27	28	41	31	Cross of the Unexpected
5389-4978 BC	The Key	35	5	63	64	Cross of Consciousness	3	50	60	56	Cross of Laws
4977-4566 BC	The Key	16	9	37	40	Cross of Planning	42	32	61	62	Cross of Maya
4565-4154 BC	The Key	20	34	65	59	Cross of the Sleeping Phoenix	51	57	54	63	Cross of Penetration
4153-3742 BC	The Key	8	14	30	29	Cross of Contagion	21	48	38	39	Cross of Tension
3741-3330 BC	The Key	23	43	49	4	Cross of Explanation	17	18	58	52	Cross of Service
3329-2928 BC	The Lock	2	1	13	7	Cross of the Sphinx	25	46	10	15	Cross of the Vessel of Love
2927-2506 BC	The Key	24	44	19	33	Cross of the Four Ways	36	6	11	12	Cross of Eden
2505-2094 BC	The Key	27	28	41	31	Cross of the Unexpected	22	47	26	45	Cross of Rulership
2093-1682 BC	The Key	3	50	60	56	Cross of Laws	63	64	5	35	Cross of Consciousness
1681-1270 BC	The Key	42	32	61	62	Cross of Maya	37	40	9	16	Cross of Planning
1269-858 BC	The Key	61	57	54	53	Cross of Penetration	55	59	34	20	Cross of the Sleeping Phoenix
857-446 BC	The Key	21	48	38	39	Cross of Tension	30	29	14	8	Cross of Contagion
445-34 BC	The Key	17	18	58	52	Cross of Service	49	4	43	23	Cross of Explanation
33 BC-378 AD	The Lock	25	46	10	15	Cross of the Vessel of Love	13	7	1	2	Cross of the Sphinx
379-790 AD	The Key	36	6	11	12	Cross of Eden	19	33	44	24	Cross of the Four Ways
791-1202 AD	The Key	22	47	26	45	Cross of Rulership	41	31	28	27	Cross of the Unexpected
1203-1614 AD	The Key	63	64	5	35	Cross of Consciousness	60	56	50	3	Cross of Laws
1615-2026 AD	The Key	37	40	9	16	Cross of Planning	61	62	32	42	Cross of Maya
2027-2438 AD	The Key	55	59	34	20	Cross of the Sleeping Phoenix	54	53	57	51	Cross of Penetration
2439-2850 AD	The Key	30	29	14	8	Cross of Contagion	38	39	48	21	Cross of Tension
2851-3262 AD	The Key	49	4	43	23	Cross of Explanation	58	52	18	17	Cross of Service
3263-3674 AD	The Lock	13	7	1	2	Cross of the Sphinx	10	15	46	25	Cross of the Vessel of Love

Source: From the teachings of the Global Consciousness Program by Ra Uru Hu, recorded and transcribed by Mary Ann Winiger (Key-To-You.com), published at Jovian Archive (JovianArchive.com)

The 510-Year Drought Cycle

Remember Professor Raymond Wheeler's 100-year climate cycles from chapter four? Well, those were sub-cycles of a larger approximately 510-520 year drought cycle that ultimately shapes not just centuries, but civilizations. These long arcs correspond to the shift in world system and turnover of the global cycle. Entire orders of power, faith, and trade rise in the warming phase, consolidate at the crest, and decline as the cold returns.

Wheeler observed that roughly every 510 to 520 years, the Earth enters a period of climatic transition marked by aridification and environmental stress. These shifts tend to disrupt agricultural stability, trigger mass migrations and invasions, and set off waves of political upheaval that dissolve one civilizational order and give rise to another. Warm phases of the cycle tend to bring growth, empire building, scientific optimism, and centralization. During cold phases resources tighten and people go on the move. Migration increases, political trust erodes, revolutions break out, and entire world systems dissolve.

He also pointed out that the particularly severe cold-dry phases align with some of the most dramatic societal shifts on record: the fifth century BCE, and the first, fifth, tenth, and fifteenth centuries CE. These are the moments when global orders shifted, empires broke apart, and entirely new social systems emerged. His summary was simple: when cold and drought reach their height, civilizations reach their breaking point.

According to his calculations, we are now entering one of those intense contraction points. This is the twenty-seventh cold-dry phase since 540 BCE, and the fifth within the current 500-year cycle. At the same time, we are nearing the climax of a thousand-year warm arc.(Wheeler believed that every second 510-year cycle reaches an extreme point, creating not just an era of hardship but the end of a much larger 1,000-year rhythm.) Historically, this combination creates a final surge of heat, instability, and hubris just before a deeper contraction sets in. Wheeler identified the year 1999 as the moment when two powerful patterns—the 170-year civil conflict cycle and the 510-year drought cycle—crossed. In his view, that intersection marked the opening note of the global unraveling we are now living through.

Wheeler also identified a recurring pattern in which each 510-year climatic shift overlaps with a transfer of economic and cultural dominance between East and West. When Greece began to wane around 670 BCE, Rome rose. As Rome faded, Eastern empires surged. When Byzantium and Asian powers declined around 450 CE, Western kingdoms began to consolidate. Nearly 500 years later, the Mongol Era signaled an Eastern resurgence. Around 1470, Europe took the lead, eventually handing that momentum to the United States. By Wheeler's logic, the pendulum is now swinging back toward the East, a shift we can already feel in the rise of China, Russia, India, and new Eurasian alliances.

Through the perspective of the drought cycle, warm eras tend to build empires and tighten control. Cold eras break those empires open and return power to the people, often through upheaval and reform. According to this model, we are nearing the crest of the current 500-year cycle, which explains the growing signs of resource tension, agricultural disruption, migration crises, and global systemic strain that echo earlier turning points in history.

Approximate Historical Peaks of the 500-Year Drought Cycle

(These dates are often given with a ±20-year buffer, as climate shifts are gradual)

Cycle	Approx. Date of Major Drought/Collapse	Civilizational Marker
3000 BCE	~3000–2900 BCE	Late Neolithic disruptions; Sahara turns from green to desert
2500 BCE	~2500–2400 BCE	Old Kingdom Egypt drought / First Intermediate Period begins
2000 BCE	~2000–1900 BCE	Collapse of Sumerian cities & Indus Valley Civilization decline
1500 BCE	~1500–1400 BCE	Minoan eruption/climate stress; migrations in Near East
1000 BCE	~1050–950 BCE	Bronze Age Collapse (Sea Peoples, fall of Mycenae, Hittites)
500 BCE	~500–450 BCE	Persian invasions, Greek upheavals, Chinese Warring States era
0 CE	~50 BCE–50 CE	Roman shift from Republic to Empire; Judean revolts
500 CE	~450–550 CE	Fall of Rome, mass migrations, Dark Ages begin
1000 CE	~950–1050 CE	Medieval Warm Period shifts, Viking expansions, feudal restructuring
1500 CE	~1450–1550 CE	Late Medieval crisis, Little Ice Age begins, European religious wars
2000 CE	**~1950–2050 CE***	Modern climate instability, water scarcity, migration waves, paradigm collapse

Astrologically, this 510-year drought cycle aligns with the Neptune–Pluto cycle, which features a conjunction between the two planets every ~492 years. Within each Neptune–Pluto cycle, there are five sub-cycles of roughly 100 years each, matching the rhythm of major geopolitical and economic realignments. The most recent Neptune–Pluto conjunction took place in 1891–1892, marking the beginning of the global industrial and financial order we still operate within today. Just as the previous conjunction around 1398 coincided with the early Renaissance, the fall of feudal power, and the beginning of European maritime expansion, the 1890s cycle reset launched the American century and the Western-dominated world economy.

If Wheeler's drought cycle and the Neptune–Pluto cycle are indeed tracking the same long-wave pattern—one through climate and one through consciousness—then we should expect the next civilizational shift to coincide with both an ecological and ideological break. In the same way Columbus' voyage marked a transfer of global trade toward the West under the last cycle, we are now witnessing an eastward economic and strategic rebalancing, along with a breakdown of the Western industrial paradigm. In this view, financial centers, power blocs, and even the mythic story of progress itself tend to migrate with the turning of these 500-year cycles—not by accident, but through synchronized shifts in environment, resources, and the underlying worldview that directs human systems.

Bottom line is that the climate is once again setting the stage for big shifts. The turbulence we're living through may not be a deviation from progress but a feature of a system returning to equilibrium. The wars, institutional breakdowns, and ideological extremes of our time echo the last great transition, when the warmth of the Renaissance gave way to centuries of conflict and reformation.

Where We Are Now: Oscillation & Prototypes

Every great system has its season. Feudalism collapsed under famine, plague, and revolt, giving way to capitalism. Carried by European empires, capitalism expanded until it hit the limits of growth and legitimacy. The nation-state rose as its political framework, and the United States became its inheritor and transformer. Now, the signs are all pointing to the twilight of that order.

What comes next isn't fixed or fated, but the outlines are emerging. Geography and demography still shape power. North America, with its resources and dual-ocean position, remains the strategic center of gravity. Yet the unipolar world is giving way to a multipolar one: regional powers like Poland, Turkey, and Japan are asserting influence, while the U.S. shifts from global manager to selective participant. China and Russia remain major players but face demographic, economic, and structural limits that constrain their reach.

At the same time, the demographic engine that fueled the modern world (ever more workers, consumers, and soldiers) has stalled. Aging populations, shrinking work forces, and fertility decline are rewriting the logic of growth. Immigration will increasingly become a global competition for people rather than a question of borders. Technology, especially AI and biotechnology, will be forced to fill the gap making productivity depend less on scale and more on innovation and adaptability.

As Immanuel Wallerstein observed, systems rarely collapse overnight; they oscillate until a new equilibrium forms. The prototypes of the next order are already visible: decentralized finance, regenerative economics, micro-communities, and sovereign individuals living across borders. Human Design frames this as the shift from the Cross of Planning (1615–2027) to the Cross of the Sleeping Phoenix—a transition from collective management to individual sovereignty and interdependence. Old institutional narratives are fading while new ones take shape: personal autonomy, ecological balance, and localized resilience.

So what might the next world system look like? Probably a patchwork:

- **Economically:** a shift from endless growth toward sustainability and resilience.
- **Politically:** from centralized nation-states toward overlapping

sovereign ties and networks.
- **Culturally:** from industrial myths of progress toward plural, ecological, and spiritual narratives.
- **Socially:** from collective dependence toward sovereign cooperation and small-scale coordination.

The old order will not disappear quietly. States will cling to control through taxation, regulation, and nostalgia. Resistance will be fierce. But the cycle is clear: endings are transitions. The end of one opens the space for another. We are not witnessing the death of history but the birth of a new world system. The question is not *if* it comes, but *how* we navigate it. And that choice, limited though it may be, still belongs to us.

7

The Outer Planets

There are planets we can see with the naked eye, and then there are the outer planets: Pluto, Neptune, Uranus, and at times Saturn and Jupiter, depending on the scale of the conversation. We've already met them in passing throughout earlier chapters, usually in connection with a specific cycle or turning point. Now we step in closer. To understand the next twenty years—and why everything feels so unstable—we need to tune into their background frequency.

The outer planets move slowly. Their orbits take decades or even centuries to complete. While the inner or "personal" planets track our everyday emotions, decisions, and desires, the outer planets act more like the stagehands of history. They change the set, dim the lights, and signal that a new act is about to begin. Their movements coincide with the rise of empires, mass revolutions, ideological awakenings, and collapses of collective myths. They do not deal with individual lives as much as with the architecture those lives take place within.

You'll notice that the astrological patterns discussed here echo the historical cycles we traced earlier. That is not a coincidence. History speaks in events, economics speaks in markets, politics speaks in institutions, and astrology speaks in planetary archetypes. They are all different languages mapping the same underlying rhythm.

What makes this moment so charged is that from 2023-2026 all four of the outer planets will be shifting into new signs. That kind of synchronized movement is rare. It signals a full-scene change in the human story and an energetic shift not seen in centuries.

- **Pluto into Aquarius (2023–2044):** Restructuring power from the top down. As hierarchies collapse, new systems rooted in technology, networks, and collective intelligence emerge. Pluto in Aquarius transforms how humanity organizes authority, information, and innovation.
- **Neptune into Aries (2025–2039):** Awakening the spiritual warrior. Dreams and ideals move from vision to action as faith, courage, and conviction collide. This is the era of movements born from belief and ideology takes the battlefield.
- **Uranus into Gemini (2025–2033):** Rewiring the collective mind. Advances in communication, media, and artificial intelligence electrify human thought, changing how we connect, learn, and perceive reality itself.
- **Saturn into Aries (2026–2028):** Tempering impulse with integrity. This is the test of action through accountability and discipline. In 2026, Saturn's rare conjunction with Neptune at the world axis grounds vision into form, marking the first blueprint of a new world order.

In the pages that follow, we'll explore each planet's archetype, the themes awakened by its new sign, and the historical echoes that reveal what happens when these forces return. This is less about prediction and more about pattern recognition. We are mapping the unseen currents now reshaping our time. By the time these outer planets complete their cycles, the world will have transformed and so will we.

Pluto in Aquarius (2023-2044)

Pluto, with its 248-year orbit, is the outermost alchemist of the solar system. It governs death and rebirth, collapse and regeneration, shadow and transformation. It tears down what is corrupt or obsolete so that something new can take its place. Pluto's presence is not gentle; it transforms through pressure, crisis, and revelation.

In mundane astrology, Pluto represents hidden power structures, wealth, control, and mass forces that reshape civilization. It exposes corruption and forces truth to the surface. Individually, Pluto initiates us into underworld journeys of shadow and rebirth. Collectively, it signals generational upheavals that transform how societies function (as we explored in chapter 3). When Pluto changes signs, it marks a generational turning point. Entire world orders rise and fall under its influence.

Transit (2023–2044)

Pluto dipped into Aquarius in March 2023, retrograded back into Capricorn, and will remain fully in Aquarius from November 2024 until 2044. This 20-year stretch is one of the most defining astrological cycles of our era.

Aquarius governs collectives, innovation, technology, rebellion, and the future. It values networks over hierarchies and collaboration over control. But when Pluto moves through Aquarius, these ideals are tested and intensified. Power reorganizes itself through technological and ideological revolutions.

This is the era when humanity's relationship to power, technology, and truth undergoes a total metamorphosis.

Collective Themes

- **Revolutionary Upheaval:** Pluto in Aquarius historically coincides with clashes between entrenched elites and emerging collective forces. Movements for freedom, equality, and reform gain momentum but also bring their own darkness.

- **Technological Power:** Aquarius rules electricity, science, and innovation. Pluto's presence here magnifies technology's influence and exposes its underbelly: AI dominance, data surveillance, biotech, and the centralization of digital control.

- **Collective Transformation:** Decentralization and grassroots movements flourish, while traditional systems collapse. This is the power of the many challenging the few, but the transition is turbulent and uneven.

- **Hidden Networks:** Expect revelations about the invisible infrastructure, or underworld, of modern life: energy grids, intelligence networks, global finance, and the algorithms that govern behavior.

- **The Shadow of Utopia:** Every revolutionary dream carries its opposite. Under Pluto in Aquarius, collective ideals can harden into dogma. What begins as liberation can slide into authoritarian control or mass conformity disguised as progress.

Years	Historical Precedent of Pluto in Aquarius
1041–1063	Religious schisms challenge church authority; power structures in East and West reorganize. Innovations like movable type in China quietly transform how knowledge spreads.
1286–1308	The Mongol Empire reaches its zenith, then fragments. Crusader states collapse. Europe's political order reshapes, giving rise to new civic institutions.
1532–1553	The Protestant Reformation fractures Christendom. Copernicus upends the cosmic order with heliocentrism. Printing and translation democratize knowledge.
1777–1798	The Age of Revolution: American, French, and Haitian revolts overthrow monarchies and birth new democratic ideals. The Industrial Revolution begins to mechanize labor and society.

Each Pluto in Aquarius era marks a revolutionary reordering of power and knowledge. Institutions fall, new systems arise, and human consciousness leaps forward *through struggle.* Belief systems are questioned, hierarchies are toppled, knowledge is redistributed, and new technologies are unleashed.

Neptune in Aries (2025-2039)

Neptune takes about 165 years to circle the Sun, spending roughly 14 years in each sign. It moves slowly, reshaping culture, art, religion, and the collective imagination as it goes.

Archetypally, Neptune rules myth, music, mysticism, and illusion. It governs our longings for beauty, transcendence, and unity but also our susceptibility to fantasy, deception, and delusion. It's the feminine, oceanic force of compassion and collective emotion and a higher octave of Venus and the Moon. When Neptune changes signs, collective ideals shift what we believe in, what we worship, and what we dream possible.

When unafflicted, Neptune grants vision, beauty, empathy, and collective compassion. When afflicted, like she is in Aries, she unleashes collapse, scandal, instability, dishonesty, martyrdom, and uprisings fueled by "us versus them" fervor.

In mundane astrology, Neptune represents *the sentiment of the people,* such as popular opinion, democratic impulses, and mass movements. Transiting the natal fourth house of a nation, Neptune stirs political feeling and popular excitement. Unafflicted, it blesses land and crops, but afflicted, it signals discredit, failure, or scandal in government. Neptune always dissolves boundaries, whether to open us to higher realities or to plunge us into chaos.

Transit (2025–2039)

Neptune first dips into Aries from March 30 to October 22, 2025, before beginning her full 14-year transit on January 26, 2026. The timing is significant: Neptune enters Aries just as Pluto settles into Aquarius (2023–2044) a pairing that hasn't been seen since the 11th century. Together, they signal a period of revolutionary change in how humanity organizes power, identity, and belief.

Aries is the fire of initiative, ruled by Mars. It's bold, direct, and driven by self-assertion. Neptune is diffuse, idealistic, and unifying. When these two energies meet, they create the archetype of the spiritual warrior or visionary pioneer. This can manifest as inspired activism and courageous vision… or as fanaticism filled with "divine purpose" and delusion.

Collective Themes

- **Reformation & Schism:** Expect upheaval within religious, spiritual, and ideological institutions. Calls for reform, exposure of corruption, and new movements seeking purity of belief are likely to arise.
- **Charismatic Leaders & Cults:** Neptune dissolves boundaries, Aries demands action. Together, they create fertile ground for charismatic leaders, mass devotion, and martyr movements.
- **Visionary Breakthroughs:** Every Neptune-in-Aries era coincides with periods of invention and exploration. The tension between imagination and initiative often sparks major leaps in technology, medicine, and communication.
- **Ideological Polarization:** Neptune magnifies empathy but also illusion. In Aries, it can inflame identity politics and "us versus them" narratives. Expect simultaneous surges of democratic uprisings and authoritarian backlash.
- **Personal Expression:** On an individual level, Neptune in Aries asks

us to live our ideals boldly and act on inspiration. But it also warns against mistaking fantasy for purpose or using spiritual language to mask personal ambition.

Years	Historical Precedent of Neptune in Aries
1042–1057	East–West Schism brewing within the Church; cracks in spiritual authority. Parallels today's Neptune–Pluto overlap (Pluto in Aquarius).
1206–1220	Rise of the Mongol Empire under Genghis Khan. Crusades expand religious fervor and conquest.
1370–1384	Church fragmentation and early Renaissance stirrings. Faith and humanism begin to diverge.
1533–1548	Protestant Reformation. The Bible translated into vernacular languages; printing press and camera obscura revolutionize communication and perception.
1697–1712	Religious schisms, Enlightenment philosophy, and scientific progress redefine power and knowledge.
1861–1875	Neptune entered Aries just as the U.S. Civil War began. Nationalist unifications (Germany, Italy), abolitionist movements, and industrial revolutions reshape society. Railroads, telegraphs, and stock exchanges connect a new world.
2025–2039	Neptune's return to Aries begins—a new cycle of spiritual and ideological reformation on a global scale.

Each Neptune in Aries visit coincides with spiritual awakenings, ideological revolutions/violence, and the birth of new worldviews.

Uranus in Gemini (2025-2033)

Uranus, with its 84-year orbit, is the awakener of the cosmos. It is the planet of rebellion, innovation, and sudden change, breaking rules, upending assumptions, and jolting the system awake. In mythology Uranus is Prometheus, the trickster who steals fire from the gods and gives it to humanity as an act that liberates us but also changes us forever.

Archetypally, Uranus governs revolt, innovation, liberation, and anything that breaks the mold. It's associated with electricity, technology, and sudden insight, which is why each Uranus cycle tends to coincide with revolutionary leaps in both consciousness and invention.

Transit (2025–2033)

Uranus enters Gemini on July 7, 2025, where it will remain until May 2033. Gemini is the mutable air sign of language, information, media, and movement, or how we think, speak, and learn. When Uranus electrifies this domain, we experience revolutions of mind and message. It's not just a change in ideas but a total reboot of how consciousness itself connects and communicates.

As we discussed in chapter five—because Uranus takes 84 years to circle the Sun, this marks a Uranus return for the United States (based on the U.S. Sibly chart). Uranus returns bring rebellion, innovation, and new orders, but a Gemini return directs that theme towards a revolution in communication, networks, and collective identity. We feel the collective pressure and demand for freedom and innovation that inevitably rewires the national identity. When Uranus moves through the zodiac, it tends to spark collective unrest and breakthroughs in whatever realm it touches:

- In **fire signs**, it ignites wars of independence and ideological crusades.
- In **earth signs**, it reshapes industry, labor, and material reality.
- In **air signs**, it revolutionizes thought, communication, and technology.
- In **water signs**, it awakens emotion, intuition, and spiritual renewal.

Uranus in Gemini is, in a nutshell, about changing the nature of our very minds through exposure to new information, conversations, education, inventions, and interventions. It challenges what we believe is "obvious," overturns mental and cultural assumptions, and floods the collective with new information and inventions. Beliefs and perspectives that once seemed immovable will shift rapidly.

At its best, this transit brings breakthroughs in understanding and unites humanity through shared knowledge. At its worst, it can scatter attention, deepen polarization, or flood us with more data than the nervous system can process. Either way, it changes what it means to *know* anything.

Collective Themes

- **Information Shocks:** Expect seismic changes in media, AI, education, and global communication. Just as the telegraph and internet rewired the information highway and collective nervous system, this cycle will rewrite how we transmit knowledge.
- **Technological Rebellion:** Radical innovations such as quantum computing, neuro-interfaces, and interplanetary communication may emerge, challenging old hierarchies.
- **Dualities & Polarization:** Gemini's shadow is division and contradiction. Uranus here may polarize societies into "information tribes," waging ideological battles through data and media.
- **Liberation Through Language:** New storytelling mediums, revolutionary literature, or voices of dissent may ignite movements. Uranus in Gemini sparks radical shifts in cultural consciousness through words and ideas.
- **Transportation Leaps:** Gemini rules travel, and Uranus here has historically coincided with aviation breakthroughs. Expect leaps in aerospace, rockets, and particularly space travel, possibly extending humanity's reach into orbit and beyond.
- Each time Uranus moves through Gemini, the world experiences a revolution in how information, technology, and human consciousness connect.

Every Uranus-in-Gemini cycle brings a revolution of mind. Communication changes and leaps forward, ideas spread like wildfire, and humanity takes another step into the future. From the printing press to the internet, Uranus in Gemini reminds us that words are power and how we use them determines the shape of the world to come.

Years	Historical Precedent of Uranus in Gemini
405–398 BCE	Fall of Athens to Sparta; Athenian democracy collapses under internal strain. Socrates is tried and executed for teaching citizens to question official narratives.
1439–1446	Gutenberg develops the movable-type printing press. Knowledge begins decentralizing beyond church and aristocratic control. Early printed pamphlets circulate new ideas rapidly.
1606–1613	The telescope is introduced; Galileo and Kepler publish work that challenges established cosmology. First news pamphlets and early newspapers appear, altering information flow.
1690–1697	John Locke publishes *Two Treatises on Government* and *Concerning Human Understanding*, shaping Enlightenment political theory. Newton formalizes physics, rationalism spreads.
1774–1781 *(with Pluto in Aquarius)*	American Revolution. *The Wealth of Nations* is published. Steam engine advances trigger early industrial capitalism. Political and economic frameworks realign.
1858–1865 *(with Neptune in Aries)*	U.S. Civil War begins. Telegraph wires accelerate communication speed. Darwin's *Origin of Species* is published. Underground rail networks and industrial infrastructure expand.
1941–1949	World War II. Radar, nuclear energy, jet engines, computers, and coded communication systems emerge. The digital and intelligence age begins alongside new global power structures.
2025–2033 *(Uranus returns to Gemini)*	Development of AI-driven communication systems, synthetic media, and decentralized networks. Legacy narratives weaken as information control shifts to distributed platforms. A new communication paradigm challenges old state and media authority.

In mundane astrology, Uranus transits through the signs also track the evolution of technology and social systems. Uranus in Aquarius (1995–2003) coincided with the rise of the internet. Uranus in Pisces (2003–2011) dissolved boundaries through social media and virtual identity. Uranus in Aries (2011–2019) ignited global uprisings and the era of individual disruption, the "startup" mentality, the Arab Spring, the rise of digital activism. Uranus in Taurus (2018–2026) is transforming agriculture and finance as evidenced by cryptocurrency, sustainability, bio-tech. When Uranus starts moving into Gemini in 2025, the focus shifts again to information, language, and consciousness: a true mental revolution.

Over the next seven years, we can expect the pace of change to accelerate beyond anything we've yet experienced. Artificial intelligence, quantum computing, neural technology, and immersive realities will stretch the boundaries of what it means to be human. But for every breakthrough, there will be instability: misinformation, propaganda, surveillance, data wars/manipulation, and the collapse of trust in shared truth. This is the *mind's crisis*: truth and illusion wrestling for control of perception. The new battlefield won't be fought on land but in the mind. Increasingly, attention will become the resource everyone is fighting over.

Gemini's dual nature will be unmistakable. The same technologies that connect us will divide us; the same networks that carry information will carry distortion. Polarization, competing narratives, and ideological fatigue could define this era. But in the same breath, Uranus in Gemini brings a mental renaissance. In other words, a shift in how we think, learn, and perceive reality itself. We might see new breakthroughs in physics, mathematics, linguistics, and consciousness studies that reframe what it means to be human in the age of machines. We could also witness the speed of technological and social change overwhelm our systems, leading to breakdowns in communication networks, power grids, and the information economy itself.

Saturn in Aries (2025-2028)

Though Saturn isn't technically one of astrology's "outer planets," it acts as the bridge between the personal and the collective. Whenever Saturn changes signs (and especially when it joins forces with one of the big players) it leaves a visible mark on history. In 2026, Saturn does both: it permanently enters a new sign and element, moving from watery Pisces into fiery Aries, while forming a rare conjunction with Neptune. This marks a major shift in how we structure power, identity, and collective will.

Saturn's 29½-year orbit makes it the cosmic taskmaster. It is the planet of boundaries, time, discipline, and responsibility, ruling the process of growing up, facing consequences, and learning what truly lasts.

In mundane astrology, Saturn represents governments, institutions, laws, and authority. On a personal level, it rules maturity, accountability, and the need to ground dreams in reality. In myth, Saturn is Cronos: the devourer of children (symbolizing the end of childish ways) but also the keeper of time and the builder of civilization. Saturn doesn't destroy for pleasure; it prunes what's immature so that wisdom can take root.

At its core, Saturn represents "will in action." It's the part of the cosmos that demands we follow through, do the work, and build the bones of reality—whether that's through labor, law, or leadership. It's the planet of cause and effect: what you sow, you reap.

Transit (2025–2028)

Saturn spends around two and a half years in each zodiac sign, returning to Aries roughly once every thirty years. Each time it enters a new sign, it brings a sober invitation to mature that arena of life. Saturn rules structure, boundaries, effort, discipline, and the kind of integrity that is earned through time and labor. Aries, by contrast, is the spark of beginnings. It is raw identity, courage, instinct, and the will to act before certainty is guaranteed.

When Saturn (the architect)steps into Aries (the warrior) something powerful happens. The impulse to move forward meets the reality of consequence. Rash action is no longer enough. This is the moment when courage requires patience. It is the training ground of the disciplined warrior, the one who does not just charge, but builds with intention. Collectively, Saturn in Aries asks us to grow up in our relationship to will and initiative. How do we begin again without repeating the same mistakes? How do we assert individuality without collapsing into ego or conflict? How do we rebuild in a way that honors what has been learned from past collapses?

Notably, Saturn enters Aries on May 24, 2025, steps briefly back into Pisces during its retrograde phase, and then re-enters Aries on February 13, 2026, where it will remain until April 12, 2028. Just days after that second entry, on February 20, 2026, Saturn will meet Neptune at 0° Aries. This degree, known as the Aries Point, marks a world axis because 0 degrees Aries is literally the start of the zodiac. Energetically, this suggests it is one of the most potent portals for collective new beginnings. Saturn meeting Neptune here signals the opening of a new chapter not only in personal identity but in the myth and structure of civilization itself.

Collective Themes (against the backdrop of Neptune in Aries)

- **Identity Under Pressure:** Saturn in Aries strips away false identities, both personal and national. We find out who we truly are when tested by reality.
- **Courage with Discipline:** Fire needs a forge. This transit demands strategy, patience, and restraint. It rewards those who act bravely but wisely, punishing impulsive or self-centered aggression.
- **Law Meets Vision:** With Neptune in the mix, religious, spiritual, and political ideals begin to harden into systems and laws. Sometimes this brings compassionate reform; other times, fanaticism roleplaying as morality.
- **Borders and Boundaries:** Saturn builds walls; Neptune dissolves them. Their dance will highlight debates over sovereignty, migration, and the balance between protection and compassion.
- **New Archetypes of Leadership:** Expect leaders who merge Saturn's discipline with Neptune's vision. This could look like spiritual movements taking political shape, or pragmatic visionaries rising from chaos. This can birth both saints and zealots.

Years	Historical Precedent of Saturn in Aries
1996–1998	Internet and globalization surge; new frontiers of communication spark debates over regulation and privacy. Clinton impeachment crisis tests authority; Kosovo conflict and nuclear tests in India–Pakistan.
1967–1969	Civil Rights reforms, Vietnam War protests, student uprisings, and assassinations—youth challenging authority. Apollo program reaches the Moon.
1937–1940	Prelude to WWII; authoritarian powers rise, League of Nations collapses, old orders crumble.
1908–1911	Industrial expansion and militarization. Labor strikes and women's suffrage movements challenge power structures. Ford's assembly line revolutionizes industry.
1878–1881	Aftermath of Russo-Turkish War; political assassinations and nationalist uprisings reshape Europe.
1848–1851	Revolutions of 1848 ignite across Europe. Old monarchies suppress them, but the seeds of democracy take hold.
1819–1821	Post-Napoleonic revolts across Europe; suppression and reform. In the U.S., the Missouri Compromise ignites slavery debates.
1789–1791	French Revolution: liberty, rebellion, and restructuring of power. The people claim sovereignty.
1759–1761	Seven Years' War reshapes global empires; Britain's dominance emerges.

Every Saturn in Aries visit brings a confrontation between force and form, will and law, freedom and responsibility.

Astrological Indications of Spring

By now you may have noticed a pattern: the planetary conditions we are entering resemble the same configurations present during the American Revolution, the U.S. Civil War, and the World Wars. It is not just that the outer planets are changing signs; it is that they are all moving into the same elemental territory at once.

For the first time in centuries, Pluto, Neptune, Uranus, and Saturn will all occupy fire and air signs at the same time. These are the yang elements associated with movement, innovation, intellect, and initiation. In contrast, the past several decades have been dominated by earth and water signatures, eras of dissolution, endurance, and structural breakdown. If earth and water represent winter, fire and air represent spring.

This elemental shift signals the ignition of a new world cycle. After a long period of institutional decay and spiritual fog, the focus now moves to creation, momentum, and the assertion of new principles. Despite how chaotic our current moment feels, the underlying energetic pattern suggests emergence rather than decline.

Each outer planet contributes a piece of this momentum. Neptune entering Aries turns vision into action and spiritual belief into movement. Pluto in Aquarius restructures civilization around networks, technology, and decentralization. Uranus in Gemini accelerates communication, thought systems, and information revolutions. Saturn in Aries brings discipline and form to new beginnings, forcing innovation to mature into responsible leadership. Their convergence *right now*, between 2023 and early 2026, marks a clear threshold moment.

The most significant marker of this shift comes when Saturn conjoins Neptune at 0 degrees Aries in February 2026, at the Aries Point, a world axis associated with collective new beginnings. This alignment marks the formal entry into a new paradigm, where vision meets structure at the degree of birth and initiation.

We could, of course, go much deeper here astrologically. We could track exact ingress times, degrees, aspects, and retrogrades. Astrology offers infinite detail for those who wish to study the sky as a science. But my goal isn't to drown us in data or lose the forest for the trees. Astrology is also an art and a language. It is a way of giving shape to energy and naming what we feel but can't quite articulate. The value of these planetary cycles is not only in their precision, but in how they illuminate the patterns beneath the experience. The shifting archetypes validate what we sense and help us adjust to how we perceive the moment. We don't need to know every minute or every orb to understand the broader current of change. What matters is learning to sense the rhythm.

The outer planets give us that astrological framing and language to explain the same vibe: the world we knew is ending, and something entirely new is taking shape. Institutions forged for the industrial age are giving way to networked, decentralized systems that behave less like pyramids and more like webs. Power is being dispersed, creation is accelerating, and the currency of the coming age is participation itself. Reputation, contribution, and resonance will replace credentials and control. Neptune in Aries dissolves the old myths of who we are; Saturn in Aries compels us to build new ones. What we're witnessing is not an apocalypse in the catastrophic sense, but in its truest meaning an *apokálypsis*, an unveiling of how power, belief, and creation truly work.

We are moving into the season of fire and air, the elemental spring of civilization. The past century's long winter of contraction is beginning to thaw. Fire brings courage, air brings vision, and together they spark the first shoots of a new epoch. Our task is to meet this convergence consciously: to channel its electricity toward creation rather than destruction, to build systems that expand freedom without losing humanity. What's being born is not just a new world, but a new way of being human within it.

To understand what this moment means just a little deeper, I invite you to zoom out one more time. This final cycle, what I have named the Epochal cycle, is a collection of myths and frameworks that once again are all saying the same thing. The backdrop of this whole Earth game is changing on a millennia long scale.

8

The Epochal Cycle

Before history was written, it was remembered in stories.

Before there were calendars or kingdoms, people marked time with the heavens. The rising and setting of the sun gave rhythm to the day. The moon's phases shaped the month. And the long, slow drift of the stars across the night sky that were hardly perceptible within a single lifetime marked something far more profound: the turning of entire world ages.

Across continents and cultures, ancient peoples understood that time wasn't linear. It moved in cycles. Spirals. Long arcs of rise and fall. And perhaps most remarkably, they agreed that human consciousness, like nature, followed that same rhythm. They knew what we are now just beginning to remember:

Civilizations have seasons. Consciousness has weather. And our history has a mythic pattern to it.

This chapter is about that pattern.

We've spent the previous chapters mapping cycles at different scales, from generational shifts to economic waves, institutional collapse to global power reconfigurations. But now, we arrive at the deepest layer of the spiral with the longest rhythm. This is the realm of the epochal cycle. It is what the Greeks called the *Great Year*, what Hindu sages called the *Yuga Cycle*, what the Maya tracked through the *Long Count*, and what modern astronomers now understand as the precession of the equinoxes.

To the ancients, this wasn't myth. It was reality. A cosmic calendar embedded into the sky, reflecting the rise and fall of human awareness. Golden Ages of clarity and alignment gave way to Dark Ages of confusion and decay not because of politics or economics, but because of a cosmic rhythm that governed the quality of consciousness itself.

This idea that humanity moves through great seasons of light and darkness is one of the most widespread and sophisticated ideas to survive from the ancient world. It appears in over thirty civilizations, from the Vedic sages of India to the astronomer-priests of Egypt, the Hopi elders of the American Southwest to the philosophers of Greece and Rome. Despite the distances between them, they shared an agreement that humanity rises and falls in rhythm with the stars.

Today, we've mostly forgotten this. Modern culture is deeply invested in the myth of progress. Of nonstop forward movement, of constant improvement, and of being the most advanced civilization to ever exist. But as the idea that *maybe we aren't the peak of civilization* starts to feel a little too true, we are becoming more open to the idea that time and evolution is not a line—it's a loop. That civilizations don't evolve in one direction forever.

This is the central insight of the epochal cycle. Not that everything gets worse. Not that everything improves. But that everything turns.

In this chapter, we'll explore how the ancients tracked that turn. Because the confusion, overwhelm, despair, and rage we're living through now is not just a crisis of systems. It's a signal that a world age is ending. That we are in a massive turning, much bigger than you or I can really comprehend, and feeling like the floor is gone is part of that experience.

The Forgotten Science of Myth

In the late 1960s, historian of science Giorgio de Santillana (MIT) and cultural historian Hertha von Dechend (University of Frankfurt) published *Hamlet's Mill: An Essay on Myth and the Frame of Time.* This book quietly upended the study of myth. Their argument was as daring as it was meticulous: that ancient myths were not merely symbolic stories or moral parables, but encoded records of astronomical knowledge.

At the heart of their thesis was the precession of the equinoxes, or the slow, rhythmic "wobble" in Earth's axis that causes the stars to shift gradually over a cycle of roughly 25,920 years. To Santillana and von Dechend, this was no obscure celestial curiosity, but a kind of hidden clock embedded in the world's mythologies. It was, and is, the great measure of time by which civilizations rise, decline, and renew.

Von Dechend's early research into Polynesian and Mesopotamian myths led her to notice peculiar patterns: temples and ceremonial sites often aligned not just with local star risings but with solstitial and equinoctial points that marked the Sun's path across the year. These alignments, she argued, hinted that cosmology was embedded into architecture, ritual, and story. Myth was not separate from science, but actually science expressed through symbol.

Working together, Santillana and von Dechend traced the same pattern across continents and eras: Babylonia, Egypt, India, Greece, Mesoamerica. Myths of gods battling, worlds flooding, or thrones overturned were, they proposed, allegories for the slow turning of the heavens. Essentially, the astronomical and metaphysical memory of sacred knowledge was retained in the collective consciousness through allegory. Over the millennia, those symbols decayed into stories, the meaning forgotten but the structure preserved. What looked like folklore concealed a sophisticated awareness of the cosmic order.

Western science formally recognized precession only in the 2nd century BCE, through the Greek astronomer Hipparchus, yet *Hamlet's Mill* suggested that earlier civilizations had not only observed it but encoded it in myth, preserving that knowledge through story long before written science. If cultures separated by oceans and millennia all carried fragments of the same cosmic cycle, then we are left with two possibilities: either these stories emerged independently, shaped by the universal sky we all share or they are remnants of a forgotten global science, an ancient awareness that the heavens themselves mark the rhythm of human time.

This cycle is near and dear to my heart because it is the one that first got me really looking at cycles back in 2020. The more I found, the more interesting it all became. (Now I can't help but notice them in every discipline, but that's another story). Though this chapter could be a book on its own, we will focus on seven cultural iterations of the Epochal Cycle to help illustrate the energy and timing of the shift that is occurring right now.

Mesopotamia: Time as Measurement

Tens of thousands of years before writing, people tracked the Moon's phases, the migration of stars, and the return of seasons. But in Mesopotamia, between the Tigris and Euphrates Rivers, this practical sky-watching evolved into something more systematic. Here, observation became record, and record became law. What began as practical observation that dictated knowing when to plant, when rivers might flood, when seasons would shift, etc. slowly became one of humanity's first systems for measuring time.

By around 2000 BCE, Mesopotamian priest-scribes were charting celestial movements on clay tablets, correlating planetary patterns with agricultural cycles, river floods, and the fate of kings. These observations were not seen as separate from governance or religion. The stars set the terms for earthly rule. Kings claimed authority not through divine favor alone, but through demonstrated alignment with cosmic order. In this world, time shifted from a natural rhythm to a structured framework—something that could be measured, interpreted, and used to organize an entire civilization.

Their famous creation story, the *Enuma Elish* (committed to writing around 1100–1200 BCE, though based on much older Sumerian material), gives us a window into this worldview. In the epic, the god Marduk rises to power by defeating the chaos dragon Tiamat. From her divided body he forms the structure of the cosmos: heaven above, earth below. But his victory is not just about creation. It is about order. After establishing the world, Marduk fixes the courses of the stars, assigns each god to a constellation, and sets the calendar in motion.

In this mythic act, time itself becomes a divine ordinance. The sky is not just a backdrop but a regulated system that defines when rituals are to be held, when kings may act, and when the people must rest or begin again. To live in harmony with the heavens was to live in alignment with divine law. To fall out of step was to invite chaos back into the world.

The Babylonians were also among the first to divide the ecliptic into twelve sections, laying the groundwork for the zodiac we still use today. Each segment corresponded to a region of the sky associated with specific deities and seasonal events. Though they may not have formally recognized the slow "wobble" of Earth's axis known as precession, their centuries of records suggest they noticed subtle shifts in the background stars over time.

Later civilizations, including the Assyrians and Chaldeans, expanded this system into a form of early astrology. They linked celestial movements to human events, interpreting eclipses, comets, and planetary conjunctions as messages from the gods. The stars were not distant or indifferent—they were part of the kingdom's governance. Kings consulted sky-watchers before making major decisions, believing that good rule depended on remaining in harmony with cosmic order.

In Mesopotamia, time was both sacred and strategic. It was a tool for aligning heaven and earth, and for keeping society in rhythm with something greater. Much of this star knowledge eventually traveled through Persia and into Greece, forming the foundation of both Western astronomy and astrology.

More than any other civilization of its time, Mesopotamia tried to turn observation into order. They took what they observe about the movements of the sky and made them measurable, predictable, and law-like. In doing so, they gave the world not just the first calendars and zodiacs, but the idea that time itself could be governed.

Vedic India: Time as Consciousness

While Mesopotamia gave the world one of its first recorded systems of measured time, Vedic India developed something different: a philosophy of time itself. The Vedic tradition is rooted in an oral lineage that likely predates many written records, yet its documented cosmology emerges historically after Mesopotamian star law. But where Mesopotamia used the heavens to regulate agriculture and kingship, the Vedic sages asked a deeper question: *What is time for?*

Earlier civilizations observed the stars to survive. The Vedic seers observed them to understand the evolution of consciousness. To them, the cosmos was not a mechanical clock but a living field of intelligence. Time was sacred, purposeful, and alive. The rise and fall of civilizations, in this view, reflected not simply climate or political change, but shifts in the collective state of human awareness.

The earliest Vedic texts reveal a world in which time itself is holy. Reality is described as rhythmic and alive, moving through vast cycles of creation, preservation, and dissolution. Time is not imagined as a straight line but as a wheel known as *Kala Chakra*, the Wheel of Time. Each revolution of this cosmic wheel ushers in a change in consciousness moving from unity to fragmentation and back again. Time, in this framework, is not merely chronology but an unfolding rhythm through which both the cosmos and human awareness evolve together.

The Vedic astronomers, or Jyotishis, were among the first to unite spiritual cosmology with precise observation. The stars were seen as expressions of divine intelligence guiding the unfolding of Dharma through the ages. Texts like the *Vedanga Jyotisha* (c. 1200 BCE) demonstrate sophisticated understanding of solar, lunar, and planetary cycles, including early recognition of precessional shifts. The *Rig Veda* (c. 1500–1200 BCE) speaks of time as cyclical and sacred, while later works such as the *Mahabharata*, the *Puranas*, and astronomical treatises like the *Surya Siddhanta* develop this into a vast architecture of cosmic ages known as the Yuga Cycle.

The Yugas form one of the world's oldest continuous cosmological systems, describing the rise and fall of human consciousness across four great ages:

Satya Yuga (Krita Yuga): *The Age of Truth*
   The golden age, when humanity lived in direct alignment with Dharma, the natural law of harmony and truth. The Vedas say this was an age of purity, health, and divine knowledge where meditation was effortless and truth self-evident.

Treta Yuga: *The Age of Ritual*
   As consciousness declined, sacred order required maintenance through ritual and devotion. This is when separation from divine oneness began.

Dvapara Yuga: *The Age of Duality*

Knowledge expanded but wisdom fractured. Technology, power, and warfare intensified. The *Mahabharata* describes this turbulent age, where Krishna (the redeemer archetype also mythologized as Jesus, Osiris, Mithras, Baldr, and others) incarnates to restore balance before the great descent.

Kali Yuga: *The Age of Darkness*

The final and densest era, when Dharma 'stands on one leg.' Greed, confusion, and spiritual amnesia prevail. Human lifespans shorten, faith weakens, and sacred knowledge is lost or distorted. According to traditional reckoning, we have been in the Kali Yuga (surprise suprise) which began around 3102 BCE, shortly after the death of Krishna.

In the classical model, the four Yugas together span a vast cycle of 4.32 million years, but not everyone agrees on these time scales. In the late 19th century, the Indian sage Sri Yukteswar, teacher of Paramahansa Yogananda, offered a more astronomically aligned interpretation. In his 1894 book *The Holy Science*, Yukteswar suggested that the Yuga Cycle corresponds not to millions of years, but to the ~24,000-year precession of the equinoxes. Drawing on ancient texts such as the *Surya Siddhanta*, he described this as a cosmic reflection of human consciousness: just as the Earth moves around the Sun, humanity, too, orbits around its own spiritual center, periodically descending into darkness and rising again toward illumination.

Yukteswar's model described two, one descending and one ascending, each lasting 12,000 years. Humanity descends gradually into materialism and ignorance, reaching its deepest, darkest point around 500 CE, before slowly ascending again toward greater awareness. In this framework, we are now emerging from the Kali Yuga into the early Dvapara Yuga, an age of energy, technology, and reawakening.

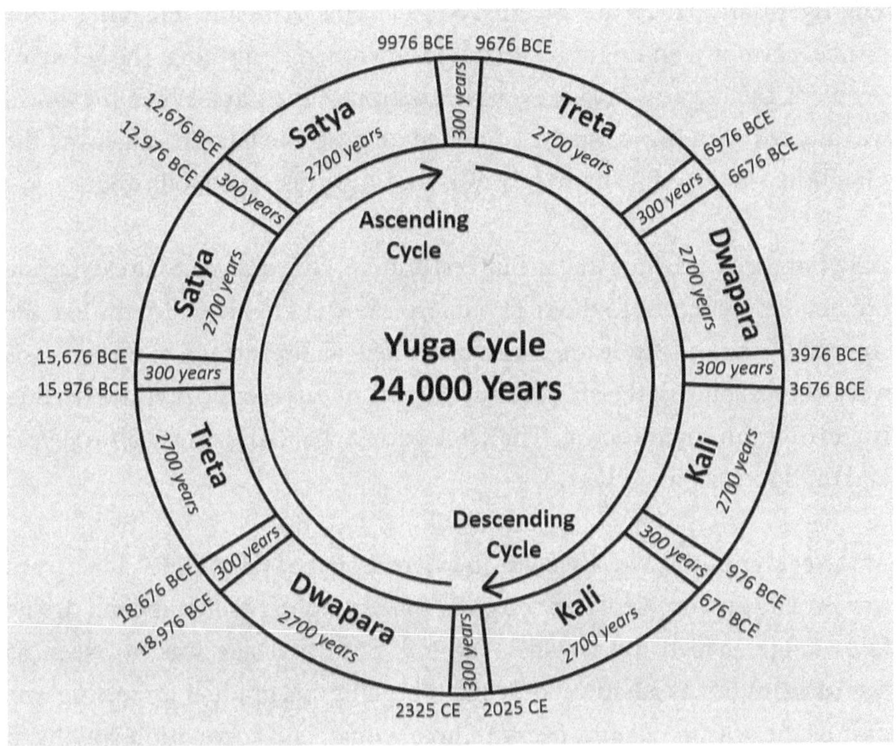

Whether one follows the long or short chronology, the symbolism remains the same: time as a sacred descent and return. The Yugas express a recognition that consciousness itself waxes and wanes in tune with the cosmos. Civilization, morality, and memory follow these rhythms.

Ancient Egypt: Time as Architecture

Where Mesopotamia measured the heavens, Egypt built them. The rhythm of the sky shaped every aspect of Egyptian life from the flooding of the Nile to the rise of kings. To the ancient Egyptian mind, the cosmos was not an abstract realm above but the living pattern beneath all things. Civilization itself was designed to stay in harmony with that pattern.

The Egyptians called this balance Ma'at. This principle, meaning truth, justice, harmony, and right relationship, governed everything: the behavior of rulers, the fairness of law, even the motion of the stars. When the world was aligned with Ma'at, the Nile flooded on time, the harvest came, and the kingdom prospered. When Ma'at was lost, disorder (*Isfet*) followed.

Egyptian time was not linear but restorative. The means that each cycle did not simply return to the start but also returned to order. Myths like the story of Osiris and his death, dismemberment, and resurrection through Isis were not just tales of the afterlife but mirrors of this cosmic rhythm: decline, fragmentation, and renewal. The same pattern guided the agricultural year and the succession of kings.

At the center of this worldview stood Zep Tepi, the "First Time." It referred to a mythic golden age when the gods walked among humanity and divine knowledge shaped the world. The fall from that age was not seen as punishment but as a natural descent. Thought this gradual forgetting was part of the season change, every temple, ritual, and coronation sought to recall Zep Tepi and restore the world to that original balance.

Much like in Mesopotamia, Egyptian astronomy was both sacred and pragmatic. Priests tracked the stars to predict the annual inundation of the Nile, to regulate festivals, and to orient temples with astonishing precision. The star Sirius (Sopdet), whose heliacal rising marked the start of the new year and the coming flood, was especially important. Temples such as Dendera were aligned to this moment, capturing the exact point on the horizon where Sirius rose just before dawn. When this happened it was a signal that the land and cosmos were once again in harmony.

The Egyptian calendar combined solar, lunar, and stellar cycles. A 365-day civil year ran alongside a star calendar that used "decans," or groups of stars rising at set intervals through the night, to mark hours and seasons. Over time, priests noticed that stellar risings drifted slightly against their civil calendar, a careful record that hints at an early awareness of what we now call precession.

This integration of astronomy, agriculture, and theology created one of history's most stable civilizations. To the Egyptians, measuring time was spiritual maintenance, and in that way it was also incredibly practical. Aligning temple walls, planting crops, and performing rituals were all acts of re-establishing cosmic order on Earth.

Their funerary texts, including the Pyramid Texts and the Book of the Dead, echoed the same logic. These were not simply guides to the afterlife but instruction manuals for realigning the soul with Ma'at and the eternal stars. The goal was not to escape the world, but to move in rhythm with it and remember one's place in the larger design.

Even after dynasties fell and new empires rose, this idea of time as sacred architecture endured. The Greeks would translate it into philosophy and Rome would turn it into law.

Greece and Rome: Time as Law

By the time Egypt entered its long twilight (and Babylonian astronomers were *still* watching the heavens), another way of thinking about time began to take shape in the Mediterranean world. In Greece and Rome, the story of the cosmos turned toward philosophy, mathematics, and law.

The Greeks inherited fragments of older star lore from Egypt, Mesopotamia, and Persia, but they reframed it through their frameworks of inquiry and logic. The sky was no longer just the realm of gods but a field of pattern and principle. The cycles of the heavens could be measured, mapped, and understood. Yet for all their rationalism, the Greeks still carried the same ancient intuition: that humanity itself moves through periods of ascent and decline as part of the larger cycle of cosmic time.

The poet Hesiod, writing in the 8th century BCE, preserved one of the oldest Greek expressions of cyclical time in his *Works and Days*. He described humanity passing through five successive ages:

- The **Golden Age**, when people lived in harmony and abundance under Kronos (Saturn), free from toil and suffering.
- The **Silver Age**, when arrogance and neglect of the gods led to decline.
- The **Bronze Age**, an age of violence and conquest.
- The brief **Age of Heroes**, marked by valor and noble struggle.
- And finally, the **Iron Age** (his own era, and ours) characterized by corruption, greed, and labor without rest.

Like the Vedic Yugas or the Egyptian Zep Tepi myth, Hesiod's Ages of Man described time as moral and spiritual descent, not historical progress. Humanity, he implied, lived through seasons of virtue and decay, ultimately returning to renewal.

A few centuries later, the philosopher Heraclitus of Ephesus (6th century BCE) deepened this view. Known for his cryptic aphorism *panta rhei*, or "everything flows," Heraclitus saw change itself as the divine law. The universe, he believed, moved through endless transformation governed by the tension of opposites: war and peace, order and chaos, creation and destruction.

According to later commentators like Censorinus, Heraclitus spoke of a Great Year. In his opinion, this was a vast cosmic cycle lasting 10,800 years, after which the universe would be consumed in a purifying fire (*ekpyrosis*) and born anew. This fiery renewal bore striking resemblance to the Yuga concept of destruction and restoration, suggesting a shared recognition that cosmic order requires periodic dissolution.

Two centuries later, around 360 BCE, Plato gave this vision its philosophical structure. In the *Timaeus*, he introduced the idea of the "Perfect Year," or the moment when all planets, the Moon, and the Sun return to their original positions, completing a single revolution of celestial time. This, he said, marked the renewal of worlds: the end of one cosmic order and the beginning of another.

For Plato, time itself was "the moving image of eternity." The heavens were the blueprint of divine intelligence, and by studying their order, humanity could remember its own. He even associated the signs of Cancer and Capricorn with the "gates" of incarnation and liberation, meaning these were the doorways through which souls entered and departed the material world. Time, then, was not just physical but metaphysical law governing the evolution of both cosmos and soul.

By the first century BCE, the Romans carried these ideas forward with their love of structure and precision. The statesman Cicero, in *De Natura Deorum*, described the Great Year as the period in which the Sun, Moon, and five visible planets complete their orbits and return to the same relative positions. He estimated its length at 12,954 years—a figure remarkably close to half the modern precessional cycle of 25,920 years.

While not scientifically exact, Cicero's calculation reflected a growing awareness that the cosmos moves in measurable patterns. With this came the assumption that human history might also follow those patterns.

From Philosophy to Astronomy

This merging of mysticism and measurement reaches a turning point with the Greek astronomer Hipparchus in the second century BCE. By comparing his own star charts with much older Babylonian records, he noticed something astonishing: the equinoxes were not fixed. Over long periods, their position drifted slowly backward through the zodiac.

This was the discovery of what we now call the precession of the equinoxes—a cycle of about 25,920 years caused by the slow wobble of Earth's axis. Hipparchus could not explain the cause, but he could measure the effect. He estimated a shift of roughly one degree every century, a remarkable insight for his time. For the first time, the Great Year of Plato and earlier mythic philosophies had a measurable astronomical basis.

Centuries later, Isaac Newton refined the rate of precession to one degree every 72 years and explained its mechanics through gravity and Earth's axial bulge. What is striking is how close this is to the symbolic encoding found in ancient temples, Vedic numerical cycles, and mythic calendars. Many ancient structures, like Egyptian temples aligned to the heliacal rising of stars like Sirius, show slight alignment drift over centuries, suggesting an awareness of precessional movement long before it was formally calculated.

In this way, the Greeks quietly closed the loop: mythic time and astronomical time were no longer separate languages. The great cycles spoken of by Hesiod, Plato, and the priest-astronomers now had a measurable counterpart in the motion of the heavens.

Hebrew: Time as Covenant

On the surface, the Hebrew Bible appears linear: a story of creation, covenant, exile, and redemption. Yet beneath that historical narrative runs a deeper current, one that reflects the same cyclical rhythm found across the ancient world.

The Hebrews inherited their cosmological framework from a broader Near Eastern milieu of Babylonian, Egyptian, and Canaanite cultures that all wove astronomy into theology. Early Hebrew culture absorbed the language of the heavens but, being the patriarchal culture they were, translated it into the language of covenant and hierarchy. The Book of Genesis describes the creation of "lights in the firmament… for signs and for seasons, and for days and years" (Genesis 1:14). This wasn't metaphorical. It reflected an understanding that celestial order was divine order.

The Hebrew calendar, still in use today, is lunisolar, blending solar years with lunar months. Its festivals mark astronomical alignments:

- **Passover** falls on the first full moon after the spring equinox.
- **Sukkot**, the harvest festival, arrives at the autumn equinox.
- **Rosh Hashanah**, the Jewish New Year, is timed to the new moon closest to that same turning point.

Even the Sabbath cycle (six days of work followed by a seventh of rest) mirrors the rhythm of the seven classical planets, which were each associated with a day of the week across Mesopotamia and later Rome. These patterns reveal that Hebrew timekeeping, though moralized through faith, was built on the same astronomical foundation as its neighbors.

In the Hebrew worldview, time was measured not only in days and years but in nested weekly, yearly, and generational cycles. The seven-year Shemitah cycle allowed the land to rest. The 49- or 50-year Jubilee restored property and freed slaves, symbolizing renewal. Prophets spoke of "times and seasons" (mo'adim) that carried divine significance. Ecclesiastes reminds us that "to everything there is a season, and a time to every purpose under heaven."

Unlike the Vedic or Hellenistic systems, Hebrew cosmology never openly named a "Great Year" or "Yuga Cycle." Instead, it encoded cosmic time in vision, allegory, and number. The Book of Daniel preserves one of the clearest examples. In his interpretation of Nebuchadnezzar's dream, Daniel describes a statue made of successive metals: gold, silver, bronze, iron, and clay, each representing a descending age of empire:

"This image's head was of fine gold, his breast and arms of silver, his belly and thighs of brass, his legs of iron, his feet part of iron and part of clay." (Daniel

2:32–33)

The symbolism mirrors the Greek Ages of Man and the Hindu Yuga Cycle: the decline from spiritual unity to material fragmentation. Similarly, Daniel's vision ends in renewal: a stone "cut without hands" that shatters the statue's base and ushers in a new kingdom. This is the logic of cyclical time: divine intervention and cosmic reset.

A similar pattern appears in Ezekiel's vision of the four living creatures, each with the face of a lion, ox, man, and eagle. To modern readers, this may sound mystical or symbolic. To ancient astronomer-priests, it was astrological. These are the four fixed signs of the zodiac that mark the equinox and solstice points: Leo, Taurus, Aquarius, and Scorpio. They form what was later called the "celestial cross," the pillars of the cosmic wheel of time. The same four symbols reappear in the Book of Revelation and in Christian art as the emblems of the four evangelists, suggesting an unbroken thread of stellar symbolism running through Western sacred tradition. Even the Twelve Tribes of Israel were symbolically linked to the twelve constellations, a pattern reflected in early synagogue mosaics where zodiac wheels frame images of the menorah or the Temple.

Though astrology later became taboo within Judaism, it was not always so. Texts like the Book of Enoch, once widely read in Second Temple Judaism, describe the stars as living beings governed by angelic intelligence, or guardians of divine order. The Dead Sea Scrolls include an *Astronomical Book* or *Book of Luminaries* (linked to the Book of Enoch) outlining a 364-day calendar based on solar cycles and equinoxes, designed to align human worship with cosmic rhythm. This calendar was intentionally solar, not lunar like the mainstream Jewish calendar later adopted by rabbinic tradition. The Qumran community believed the lunar calendar had become corrupted and fallen out of alignment with divine time. In their view, to be out of sync with the heavens was to be out of sync with covenant, a direct echo of the Mesopotamian idea that cosmic order establishes social and spiritual order.

This hidden cosmology carried forward into early Christianity. The life of Christ itself follows the rhythm of the heavens. His symbol is the fish (Ichthys) and his disciples are "fishers of men." His ministry coincides with the dawn of the Age of Pisces, symbolized by the fish, and corresponding to the zodiacal age that began around the first century BCE. Opposite Pisces lies Virgo, the Virgin, the archetypal mother through whom the savior is born. In this way, the story of Jesus is not only theological but also an astronomical marker of precession and the great turning of the ages.

Traces of this cosmic worldview still exist in modern Christianity, though most people don't realize it. The Christian liturgical calendar follows the rhythm of the Sun's movement through the solstices and equinoxes. The cross, now seen primarily as a symbol of suffering and salvation, was first a reflection of that older cosmic pattern. Even the idea of resurrection, or the story of death followed by new life that appears in nearly every ancient culture, reflects the same natural and celestial cycles our ancestors observed in the changing seasons and the movement of the stars.

Over centuries of exile, empire, and theological reform, this sky language was gradually obscured. Babylonian astronomy became "pagan." Greek astrology became heresy. Though modern faith often forgets its cosmic origins, the architecture remains. Beneath every Sunday mass and every Easter sunrise is the belief that human life unfolds in harmony, or tension, with the larger order of creation.

Mesoamerica: Time as Renewal

Between about 1000 BCE and 900 CE, while Babylonian priests were charting the planets and Greek philosophers were debating the harmony of the cosmos, a parallel vision of time was taking shape across the ocean. In the valleys and rainforests of Mesoamerica, the Olmec, Zapotec, Maya, and later the Aztec civilizations were quietly developing some of the most sophisticated astronomical systems in the ancient world.

The Olmecs, often called the mother culture of Mesoamerica, were already aligning their ceremonial centers with the Sun by around 1000 BCE. The Zapotecs continued this work at Monte Albán, where temples and plazas were designed to track the solar year. Out of this long lineage emerged the Maya, whose astronomer-priests brought these ideas to extraordinary precision during their Classic period, between about 250 and 900 CE.

Without telescopes or contact with the "Old World," the Maya created a system of mathematics, astronomy, and calendar keeping that rivaled anything known at the time. They predicted eclipses, tracked the cycles of Venus, and built pyramids aligned to solstices, equinoxes, and the rising of specific stars.

At the center of this worldview was the Long Count calendar, a base-20 mathematical system capable of recording dates that spanned thousands of years. While the 260-day Tzolk'in calendar governed ritual life and the 365-day Haab' calendar guided agriculture, the Long Count measured something larger: the unfolding of world ages.

According to Mayan tradition, humanity has passed through four previous worlds, each ending in destruction and renewal. We now live in the fifth world, which began after the last great transition. Each world age lasts about 5,125 years, and five of these together form a complete cycle of roughly 25,625 years (nearly identical to the 25,920 year precession of the equinox). That parallel is remarkable. Without any known connection to India, Egypt, or Babylon, the Maya identified the same grand rhythm of creation and renewal.

Their cities, from Tikal to Chichén Itzá, were not only political centers but architectural calendars. At Chichén Itzá, the pyramid of El Castillo casts a serpent-shaped shadow down its stairway each equinox, symbolizing the return of the feathered serpent god Kukulcán, known to the Aztecs as Quetzalcoatl. The entire city was synchronized with the heavens. To the

Maya, timekeeping was not an abstract science but a sacred duty required to live in balance with the cosmos.

Much later, the world rediscovered this system through the misunderstood 2012 phenomenon. Far from predicting the apocalypse, December 21, 2012 simply marked the end of one baktun, or 5,125-year cycle, and the beginning of another. For the Maya, this was not the end of the world but the turning of one cosmic season into the next.

The Aztecs, who inherited much of this astronomical tradition, told a similar story through the Legend of the Five Suns, or five successive worlds, each destroyed and reborn through elemental forces:

1. The First Sun (Nahui-Ocelotl) was devoured by jaguars.
2. The Second Sun (Nahui-Ehécatl) was swept away by hurricanes.
3. The Third Sun (Nahui-Quiahuitl) was consumed by fire from the sky.
4. The Fourth Sun (Nahui-Atl) was drowned in floodwaters.
5. The Fifth Sun (Nahui-Ollin) is the current age, destined for transformation through movement and earthquakes.

Each ending was not punishment (as dictated by the Hebrew tradition through the story of Noah), but a necessary cosmic correction meant to restore balance between humanity and the divine order. That understanding still endures. Across Mexico and Central America today, descendants of the Maya continue to keep the 260-day sacred calendar, using it to guide ceremonies, planting, and community life.

Indigenous North America: Time as Ceremony

Among the Hopi, Lakota, Iroquois, and countless others, time was counted through story, song, and ceremony. Their calendars were the seasons and their clocks were the stars, the animals, the rivers, and the cycles of planting and harvest.

The concept of world ages appears here too, though not written in carved tablets or astronomical calculations. Among the Hopi, one of the oldest continuous cultures in North America, oral teachings describe the unfolding of four worlds. Each world ended when humanity lost balance with nature and spirit, and each was renewed through an act of purification. The First World ended by fire, the Second by ice, the Third by flood, and the Fourth (the one we live in now) will eventually give way to the Fifth World, a new age born through restoration rather than destruction.

These transitions were similarly not seen as divine punishment but as natural repercussions of getting out of balance. The transition between worlds is meant to restore harmony between human beings and the Earth. In Hopi prophecy, the Fifth World will not emerge through technology or conquest but through remembrance. By returning to balance, to sacred law, and to the understanding that time itself is ceremonial.

In Lakota tradition, the Sacred Hoop, or medicine wheel, represents the continuous turning of life from east to south to west to north, through birth, growth, death, and renewal. Each direction carries an element, a season, and a stage of life. Time, in this view, does not advance along a line, but turns.

Among the Haudenosaunee (Iroquois), time is woven into the Great Law of Peace, one of the oldest democratic systems in the world. According to tradition, the Peacemaker arrived during a period of chaos and violence to restore unity among the nations. His teachings established not only a political confederacy but a cycle of council, renewal, and gratitude that continues to this day. The Iroquois ideal of acting with care for the next seven generations expresses this same sense of time as continuity and responsibility.

For many Indigenous traditions, time is not something to measure but something to listen to. The land speaks, the seasons shift, the animals move, and greater story is passed down through generations. This way of knowing recognizes that time is alive and human beings are participants within a larger rhythm, not observers standing outside of it.

Although colonization and forced assimilation attempted to erase these ways of knowing, they have endured. The Hopi say, "We are the ones we've been waiting for." In a time when the modern world feels uncertain and the old systems begin to fall apart, I see these teachings not as relics of the past, but instructions for how to walk through the end of one world and into the beginning of another.

Precession of the Equinox: The Cosmic Clock Beneath It All

We've now crossed continents and centuries, tracing how civilizations from Vedic India to Egypt, Greece, and the Americas. Each telling the same story in their own language: that humanity moves through repeating cycles of rise and fall, forgetting and remembering, darkness and renewal. The Yugas of India, the Egyptian Zep Tepi, the Ages of Man in Greece, and the Mayan worlds of creation and destruction all pointing to the same underlying pattern.

What if these weren't just myths or metaphors, but descriptions of a real, physical rhythm written into the fabric of the Earth itself? In my view, they are. And that rhythm is known as the precession.

Imagine a spinning top as it begins to slow down. Its axis starts to trace a wide, lazy circle. Earth does the same thing. Over thousands of years, the planet's axis slowly wobbles due to gravitational forces (mostly from the Sun and Moon tugging unevenly on Earth's not-quite-spherical shape). This gentle torque causes the direction of the axis to drift, like a slow, cosmic spiral.

The result is that the position of the equinoxes shifts. In astrological framing, it moves backwards through the zodiac at a rate of approximately 1° every 72 years. This means that the constellation behind the vernal equinox (the spring sunrise) gradually changes, moving through all twelve signs of the zodiac over a full cycle. In modern astronomy science measures precession at 25,772 years. But ancient cosmologies rounded it to 25,920. They got this number from sacred proportions (360 × 72 degrees—a symbolic perfect degree). The difference between them is only 148 years, less than one human lifetime. This suggests that the ancients were not guessing, but translating cosmic cycles into symbolic, ritual numbers that were easy to encode in myth, architecture, and sacred texts.

Every 2,160 years, we enter a new Astrological Age, or era when that vernal equinox rises in a new sign. These are sometimes called Great Months, each colored by the archetype of its corresponding zodiac sign. They unfold like cosmic seasons, each one shaping the myths, values, institutions, and worldview of the people living within it. To understand what each age meant, ancient astrologers looked to the zodiac. The Ram, the Fishes, the Water-Bearer…each sign offered a symbolic curriculum for humanity's evolution. ***For a full run down of the ages through each sign, go to appendix A.**

Right now, we are between the age of Pisces and Aquarius. (*Sidenote*: because the precession is a gradual energetic drift, not a single event, there's no universally agreed start or end date. Most astrologers frame it between 100 BCE- 100 CE through 2100-2300 CE. Either way, transitions between ages overlap for at least a century or two, placing us in the liminal period between Pisces and Aquarius.)

The Age of Pisces (~0 BCE-2160 CE) gave us mysticism, martyrdom, and mass belief. It taught us to surrender, to dissolve, to seek salvation beyond the self. It was an age of sacrifice and longing, of churches and empires, of illusion and spiritual devotion. But that age is ending and its myths are unraveling. The old gods and heroes (given to us in the Axial age) are being transformed into a version that resonates with the energy of the incoming age: Aquarius.

The Age of Aquarius promises Aquarius themes (like what we discussed when referencing Pluto in Aquarius): rebellion, revelation, and radical reorientation. This age carries the frequency of Uranus, the planet of disruption, breakthrough, and innovation. Aquarius does not ask us to pray. It asks us to wake up.

Where Pisces dissolves, Aquarius electrifies. Where Pisces asks us to believe, Aquarius demands that we see with new eyes.

Aquarius is the *water bearer* that Jesus (the master of metaphor) told us was coming next.

"Look for the man carrying the water jar" Luke 22:10

This is the age of networks, of decentralization, and of the sovereign individual inside the global collective. A time of remembering forgotten knowledge, integrating ancient wisdom with cutting-edge science, and rebuilding our systems from the ground up. Aquarius pours direct revelation into the mind. No priest, temple, or middleman required.

And like every age change, this one doesn't happen overnight. The precession is not a switch flipping but an energetic tide that takes centuries to ingress. Right now, the Piscean age is still clinging to power as evident in our belief systems, media, widespread moral/emotional manipulation and our endless yearning for saviors. But the Aquarian frequency is rising. We are getting glimpses of it in our technologies, our decentralized communities, and our collective remembering that we can think for ourselves.

You can notice the earliest moments when the frequency of Aquarius started to come into play with Scientific Revolution, the Enlightenment, and the rise of individualism in the 17th and 18th centuries. This energy has accelerated exponentially in recent decades. The internet, for example, is one of Aquarius's expressions. It is designed to connect us across time and space, to dissolve borders, and to democratize knowledge. Look at the impact it has had on us in the last few decades. That is more of what we can expect to see as time continues.

But trust me, it's not all ~golden age~ nonsense. Aquarius, like all signs, holds both medicine and madness. Its highest expression is visionary. It imagines a world where autonomous individuals collaborate in networked constellations of shared purpose. Where science and spirituality are no longer in conflict, but part of the same quest for truth. Where consciousness is not an afterthought, but the core technology. In this future, we may rediscover energy-based sciences, subtle systems of healing, and the fractal intelligence that underpins all life.

But we are not guaranteed that outcome.

Aquarius also carries the risk of depersonalization and valuing systems over souls, efficiency over empathy, and ideology over lived truth. If left unexamined, its shadow could lead us into a world of digitized control, artificial intimacy, and techno-utopian conformity that leaves the human spirit behind. The same tools that could liberate can also be used to divide, distract, and deceive. Aquarius brings both light and distortion. Its shadow wears the mask of progress: uniformity disguised as unity, surveillance disguised as safety, and authoritarianism disguised as innovation.

When thinking about where we are now and where we are headed, we have to understand that realistically both light and dark will express themselves. Duality is the nature of this three-dimensional world we are limited to perceiving. While many hinge all their hopes on the second coming of Christ, a political party or leader, or the new age assurances of moving to the 5D—these are all relics of that Pisces escapism tendency.

What's happening is that we are shifting ages. It will be better in some ways, worse in others, but all in all, it will simply be different.

Golden Age Memory and the Myth of Decline

Threaded through nearly every story of collapse is a memory of something better. A time when humanity lived in closer harmony with nature, with the divine, and with one another. Whether that memory is literal, archetypal, or both, it shows up everywhere: the Egyptians remembered *Zep Tepi*, the "first time"; the Norse spoke of a golden age of peace before the gods fell into strife; many Indigenous traditions recall earlier worlds where balance was intact before corruption set in. These weren't just nostalgic fables. They were reminders of what alignment feels like.

But the memory casts a long shadow. As cycles descend into confusion or disconnection, the echo of that earlier wholeness lingers, turning into myth, then longing, and eventually a chronic sense of loss. We see it today in the endless yearning for a simpler past, or in the fantasy that salvation lies in returning to what once was. This is what psychologists might call a "Golden Age complex," or the belief that the best has already been, leaving the present irredeemably fallen. It can paralyze us, trap us in nostalgia, and keep us from engaging with the world that's actually being born.

I'm not pretending to know the answer here, but what if the Golden Age was never meant to be a destination we could preserve or return to? What if it was meant to be a memory carried forward like a seed inside of us, waiting to be reawakened in a different season of the great spiral? What if the Golden Age isn't a place, but a *frequency*? A state of being that we all have access to and can all learn to embody (or at least visit once in a while).

Apocalypse then, in this sense, is not about losing paradise but shedding the false paradises we've built in its place. The work is not to go back, but to remember the elevated frequencies *already and always available to* us and bring them forward into a new form. The Golden Age was never meant to be preserved in stone but remembered in the soul and reawakened as the cycle turns.

Apocalypse as a Portal

When most of us hear the word "apocalypse," we think mushroom clouds, zombies, or an end-of-the-world countdown clock. But that's a modern gloss.

The original Greek word *apokálypsis* means unveiling or revealing what's been hidden.

The Aztecs spoke of Five Suns, each destroyed by catastrophe only to be followed by the birth of a new sun, a new age of humanity. The Hopi tell of earlier worlds lost to fire, ice, and flood, with survivors guided into the next one to carry forward the lessons. In India, the Yuga cycle turns with the collapse of one age and the rebirth of another, each descent preparing the ground for renewal. Even the familiar story of Noah ends not just with flood, but with covenant marking the start of a new order.

Seen through this lens, apocalypse is not just annihilation but an initiation. It is the reset built into the system to maintain balance. It is the moment in the story where the main character descends to the underworld where they are forced to shed everything that is no longer needed.

This is the moment Inanna is stripped of her jewels, Orpheus searches for Eurydice, Persephone crosses into Hades. All must endure loss before they can return with new vision. Collective cycles are no different. When civilizations unravel, when institutions crumble, when the world no longer feels familiar, we are not being punished.

We are being initiated.

This is why the stories always leave survivors. Noah with his ark. Deucalion and Pyrrha with their vessel. Manu guided by the fish. The Hopi carried into the next world. The pattern is not complete annihilation but the carrying of memory across the threshold. The ark is not just a structure of wood; it is the vessel of consciousness itself, preserving what must endure while everything else dissolves.

To see apocalypse as portal is to recognize that endings are passages. The descent strips us bare, but it also delivers us to a different horizon. What we remains becomes the foundation of the world to come. Apocalypse is the underworld we pass through on the way to remembering who we are.

As we enter the new age, and the spring of all the cycles we have discussed, we are called to step forward not just as survivors, but as co-creators. We are the stewards of what is coming. The world we are building will not be dictated by the remnants of old structures; it will be co-created by all of us, at the level of collective consciousness.

The question isn't what will happen to us, but what will we build next?

All moons, all years, all days, all winds
Reach their completion and pass away
Measuring in the time in which we can know
The benevolence of the sun
Measured in the time in which the grid of the stars looks down upon us
And through it, keeping watch over their safety
The spirits, abiding within the Stars
Measure their fate.

From the Popul Vuh, or Mayan Book of Council

9

The Quantum Paradigm

A mood of universal destruction and renewal... has set its mark on our age. This mood makes itself felt everywhere, politically, socially and philosophically. We are living in what the Greeks called the Kairos, the right moment for a metamorphosis of the gods, of the fundamental principles and symbols. This peculiarity of our time, which is certainly not of our conscious choosing, is the expression of the unconscious human within us who is changing. Coming generations will have to take account of this momentous transformation of if humanity is not to destroy itself through the might of its own technology and science. so much is at stake and so much depends on the psychological constitution of the modern human.

—Paraphrased from C.G. Jung, particularly "The Undiscovered Self" (1957) and lectures on the transformation of the gods

At the deepest levels, what it means to be human is changing. Slowly, silently(ish), but surely. We are moving into a new age and a new paradigm. The cycles we've traced in this book are not abstract curiosities but the foundation of the matrix holding everything together. Each wave, each rhythm, and each planetary passage helping to usher the new world in.

Before we look ahead, let's recap the vast amount of territory we've covered to remember where we are in time.

Multiple major and minor cycles—astrological, historical, and energetic—are converging in this decade. These are not coincidences. They are layers of the same pattern: endings, beginnings, and the reorganization of life at every scale:

- Solar Cycle 25 maximum (~2025)
- Pluto moves in Aquarius (2023-2044)
- New K-wave starting (~2030-2080)
- Saturn-Uranus conjunction (2032)
- Saturn-Pluto opposition (2035-2036)
- 17.7-year "minor war" cycle peak (2022)
- 53.5 year "major war" cycle peak (2024-2025)
- ~100 year "general war cycle" peak (late 2020s-early 2030s)
- ~100 year climate cycle in warm-dry phase (~2005-2035)
- Saeculum winter turns into Spring (late 2020s-early 2030s)
- New Political-Institutional cycle begins (late 2020s-early 2030s)
- Saturn moves into Aries at 0 degrees (2025)
- Uranus moves into Gemini (2025)
- Neptune moves into Aries (2026)
- Pluto natal return to Capricorn for US (2022-2024)
- Human Design Global Incarnation Cross Shift (2027)
- World System cycle turnover (~2000)
- Wheeler's Drought Cycle Peak (~2000)
- Move from Kali to Dwapara yuga (~early 2000s)
- Precession of the Equinox from Pisces to Aquarius (~2160)

Bottom Line: ***we are in a period of accelerated transformation.***

This is the point this book has been leading to. We are living in a moment where many cycles civilization are turning over at once. The institutions that defined the modern era, such as our governments, markets, education, media, religion, are no longer able to hold the complexity of the world they helped create. The systems that once promised stability are revealing their fragility, and the structures built to centralize power and information are transforming.

This is not simply a political or technological shift. It is a reorientation of human consciousness itself. The old story of dependence on external authorities is giving way to a new demand for participation, agency, and coherence. What once moved slowly over generations is now accelerating into a single lifetime. The world is decentralizing, not just in terms of power, but in terms of meaning. Instead of a single narrative, we face a landscape of many truths, many nodes, and many centers of gravity.

We are all together right now, crossing a threshold where collapse and creation exist side by side. Old identities are breaking apart, yet entirely new ways of organizing life are beginning to surface through experimentation, small networks, and unexpected alliances. What looks like disorder from above is, at ground level, the emergence of a new pattern—one defined less by control and more by resonance.

This moment invites a different kind of responsibility. Not the responsibility of compliance, but of *alignment*. We are being asked to participate in the creation of new forms rather than wait for new authorities to build them for us. The world ahead will not be held together by central structures, but by the integrity of individuals who know how to anchor truth in their own lives and move in rhythm with something deeper than policy or prediction.

In a single buzzword, the future is about **sovereignty**.

In every previous civilization shift, humanity had to renegotiate its relationship to power, to time, to the sacred, and to one another. That is the work before us now. The external signs of change are only the surface expression of a deeper current moving through consciousness. The question is no longer whether change is coming, because it most certainly is and there is no "going back," but how will we meet it? Will it be with fear and nostalgia, or with clarity, imagination, and the courage to build something worthy of the next world?

This book, and chapter, are here to encourage you to do the latter.

There's also something different about this turning that I believe is on our favor. We are becoming aware of awareness itself. We understand now (because our consciousness is shifting) that the universe is not a static machine but a living, participatory field that responds to said consciousness. In that sense, prediction is not fate but probability. It's a glimpse of what could unfold if current energies continue in motion. But consciousness changes the field. At any moment, through choice and awareness, we can alter the trajectory. The future is fluid, shifting with every choice, every moment of coherence, every act of attention.

So, while the cycles tell us the energetic weather ahead, how those energies take form is still up to us. Archetypes always exist on a spectrum. We can embody their higher expression or fall into their shadow. The choice, as always, is ours.

The Quantum Paradigm

If the old world was built on linear logic, control, and external validation, the emerging one is defined by a different kind of intelligence. One that moves through relationship, frequency, and alignment rather than force. We are shifting into what I call the quantum paradigm. It is not a technology or a theory, but a way of perceiving reality that changes how we act within it.

At its core, the quantum paradigm is a movement from:

- external authority → inner sovereignty
- productivity → presence and resonance
- linear thinking → intuitive knowing
- domination → collaboration
- centralization → decentralization

Main Principles

They say trying to predict the future is foolish. But I have the mic, and I know you are curious or already thinking through your own predictions anyway, so I'm going to throw my hat in the ring. Up to this point, I've done my best to stay objective while mapping the cycles. But from here on out, we move into my personal synthesis: how I see these patterns converging, and what I believe they're pointing us toward over the next century or so.

From separation to interconnection

The previous paradigm was built on hierarchy, control, and separation. It taught us to see ourselves as divided from God, from nature, from one another, and even from our own inner knowing. This worldview reached its peak in the modern industrial era, where mechanistic materialism and capitalism encouraged us to see the world as a collection of separate parts. That perspective brought significant breakthroughs such as the scientific method and global cooperation, but it also fractured our sense of belonging. Many people now feel disconnected, isolated, and unsure of where they fit within the whole.

A new paradigm is emerging. Interest in quantum science, frequency-based healing, and relational fields reflects a shift in how we understand reality. Classical physics focused on matter, certainty, and linear cause and effect.

Quantum research reveals a universe built on probability, entanglement, and the influence of consciousness. What many ancient traditions already knew, that life is woven through relationship and energetic exchange, is being remembered in new language.

We see this shift reflected in cultural movements around somatic healing, psychedelics, holistic medicine, and ecological awareness. Even our technologies mirror this transition. The internet, once viewed simply as a tool, now behaves like a living network. AI and biotechnology function through feedback and adaptation, forming something that resembles a planetary nervous system. The question is no longer whether everything is connected. The question is whether we will engage with that connection consciously.

Technology as a Mirror and Tool

We are living through an astonishing moment. Ordinary people now hold in their pockets tools that would have looked like straight-up sorcery to our great-grandparents. Artificial intelligence, genetic engineering, renewable energy, and space infrastructure are not just tools that expand human capability but mirrors. They reveal how we think about intelligence, healing, creativity, and power, reflecting back the level of consciousness interacting with them.

AI is a clear example. It is not an all-powerful, ominous godhead rising to replace us. It is a reflection of our collective psyche, showing us our values, our biases, and our fears. This is why inner coherence and discernment matter so much in this era. Our consciousness will shape how these tools are used.

Every major shift in human civilization has been catalyzed by technology. The transition from bronze to iron reshaped agriculture, warfare, and political systems. The steam engine launched industrialization and reorganized entire populations. Electricity and oil defined the twentieth century, bringing both prosperity and war. The internet collapsed distance and reshaped economies in a single generation. Now, AI is forcing us to rethink what intelligence is. Biotechnology invites new questions about what it means to be human. Renewable energy and space exploration change how we see our place in the larger system of Earth and beyond.

Technology has always been an evolutionary mirror. Life adapts by rewriting its own code, and now we can see that process happening in real time through CRISPR, gene therapies, and epigenetics. At the cultural level, technology externalizes our inner world. The internet became a global psyche where our creativity, trauma, shadow, and brilliance all play out in public view. AI now functions as oracle, mirror, and trickster, depending on who is using it and for what purpose.

The question is not whether technology will shape us. It already has. The real question is how consciously we will shape it in return. We can use it to reinforce old patterns of control or to build systems based on reciprocity and shared intelligence. Technology is not our fate. It is a reflection. What we see in it will depend on the quality of attention we bring.

Feminine Spirituality and Embodied Wisdom

This is about energetic principles, not biological gender. The paradigm we are leaving prioritized linear time, hierarchy, conquest, and productivity. It emphasized external achievement, logic, and control, which represent a distorted expression of the masculine principle. Anything intuitive, relational, cyclical, or receptive was labeled feminine and dismissed as irrational or weak.

A correction is now underway. The feminine principle is resurfacing across culture in many forms: through the recovery of suppressed histories, renewed interest in cyclical living, the rise of somatic therapies, and a return to earth-based spiritual practices. Rest, intuition, regeneration, and embodiment are no longer seen as optional but are increasingly recognized as necessary for health, sanity, and cultural resilience.

This is not about replacing one polarity with the other. We are not swapping out the dude at the top with a woman and calling it "matriarchy" (which would be inaccurate to say anyway). It is about integration. Both masculine and feminine energies have been distorted under the patriarchal paradigm. The masculine calcified into domination, and the feminine collapsed into passivity. The work now is to restore balance so that social structure can support life rather than suppress it, and intuition can inform action instead of being dismissed.

Every major turning in history has involved a return to the feminine current because cultural renewal begins in the unseen realm before it takes form. Mystical traditions, goddess lineages, and earth-centered wisdom have always reappeared when the chaos level reaches a certain pitch. We are in another one of those moments now. The void, the womb, the in-between space we find ourselves in is not a dead zone. It is a place of gestation. What emerges next will depend on how well we allow the feminine principle to re-enter and resacralize the story of being human.

Consciousness at the Center

Perhaps the most radical shift underway is the recognition that consciousness is not merely a byproduct of the brain, but the very substrate of reality itself. The realization that we are not passive observers of a mechanistic universe but the dreamers dreaming the dream. Healing, creation, and innovation are being re-understood not as acts of rearranging matter, but as processes of tuning and aligning with consciousness itself. We are finally remembering that manipulating matter is like rearranging furniture in your room when what you really need is to move to another country.

Ancient wisdom has long pointed here. Hinduism spoke of Indra's Net, an infinite web of jewels where each reflects the whole. The Vedas declared *Nada Brahma,* or that the universe is sound. Taoist texts described the Tao as the ineffable field behind all form. Genesis describes God speaking the world into being *"And God **said**, 'Let there be light"* showing reality as born of sound, not substance. Mystical traditions across cultures insisted that reality is vibration, pattern, resonance. Modern science, after centuries of materialism, is catching up on the same insight: quantum fields underlie matter, particles behave as probabilities, cymatics shows sound shaping form, and holographic models of the universe suggest that each part contains the whole. Myth and science, estranged for the last paradigm, now echo each other.

Our current apocalypse (unveiling) strips away illusions so that reality can be seen more clearly. What collapses in our time is not just political or economic systems, but the worldview that reality is dead matter, separable and inert. What emerges is recognition that reality is alive, relational, and responsive. The apocalypse is not only an ending but a chance to adjust what we are in resonance with, and therefore what kind of world we generate. This is the invitation of the quantum paradigm: to live as if the universe is alive, responsive, and participatory. Because it is.

The principles I've just outlined are the overarching energetic patterns shaping the century ahead. But principles alone can feel abstract. You might be able to sense them, but also not really understand what they might mean for your life or community. To bring them down to earth, it helps to trace how these currents might actually unfold in lived reality. What might all of this look like in our lifetimes?

Here are a few categories out of many:

Work and Success

The way most of us think about "success" today, like climbing the corporate ladder, the 9–5 grind, trading your energy for a promise of security, was never the human norm. Those ideas are recent inventions born in the industrial and postwar era. Factory whistles, punch clocks, and office towers trained people to measure life in hours, productivity, and titles. For one brief century, "success" was defined by stability and comfort: pensions, benefits, middle management, a single-family home, and retirement by age 65.

But for most of human history, work has looked very different. Farmers, artisans, healers, sailors, merchants, blacksmiths, and midwives lived more like freelancers than employees. Their livelihoods were cyclical and seasonal, shaped by harvests, festivals, and markets. Reputation, skill, and community networks mattered more than job titles. From medieval Europe's guild system to early America's patchwork of farms and small shops, small-scale, independent enterprise was the backbone of survival. Even in empires, vast numbers of people worked outside official hierarchies, adapting quickly to crises, opportunities, and local needs.

We are circling back to an older pattern of livelihood, one that looks less like corporate hierarchy and more like self-directed craft. Traditional jobs no longer offer the security they once promised, and for many, they no longer feel meaningful. In their place, we see the rise of entrepreneurship, freelance work, and small niche enterprises built around personal expertise or passion. Remote and hybrid work have erased the old boundary between home and profession, while digital platforms now allow individuals to reach global audiences without institutional backing.

Success is beginning to shift away from status and title toward freedom, flexibility, and alignment with one's own values and rhythm. The arrival of AI accelerates this even further. Most industries will either transform entirely or disappear, and the old gatekeeping systems where authority belonged to those with credentials, titles, or white coats are dissolving. With easy access to powerful AI tools, a single curious and critically thinking person can now learn, build, and solve problems once reserved for experts and institutions.

What feels new is, in fact, the original. For most of human history, people worked not as cogs in a system but as adaptive, creative, self-directed contributors because they had to be. The decline of the corporate ladder is not the end of work; it is the return of work to its more classic form. Success in the coming century will be measured less by how high we climb inside someone else's structure and more by how aligned and free we can be in our lives. The era of waiting to be granted permission is ending. The era of sovereign creators is beginning.

Health and Wellness

We have grown up in a world where the dominant view of the body has been mechanical: a collection of parts and systems, each understood in isolation and "fixed" with the right drug or surgery. Illness was treated reactively, often with a "pill for every ill." Care and knowledge was out-sourced to experts and industries (namely doctors, hospitals, pharmaceutical companies) while ordinary people were largely taught to see their bodies as mysteries they could neither fully understand nor manage.

But this too was an anomaly in the long arc of human history. For millennia, healing was communal and largely home-based. Families relied on midwives, herbalists, shamans, and folk healers. Every culture developed its own systems of integrative knowledge—Ayurveda in India, Traditional Chinese Medicine, Indigenous plant medicine in the Americas, Greco-Arabic humoral theory. People understood health not as isolating symptoms but as balancing systems: body, spirit, environment. Even in the West, until the rise of modern biomedicine in the 19th and 20th centuries, households managed the vast majority of care themselves with herbs, food, prayer, ritual, and local healers.

The industrial age revolutionized medicine: germ theory, antibiotics, anesthesia, X-rays, and advanced surgery saved countless lives. But with these successes came a narrowing of focus. The body was treated like a machine with symptoms managed in isolation rather than understood as signals from a whole system. Pharmaceutical interventions expanded rapidly, often outpacing deeper questions of prevention, lifestyle, or root cause. This narrowing was not only cultural but financial. The Rockefeller

Foundation's massive investments in the early 20th century standardized medical education and prioritized pharmaceutical, hospital-based approaches, while outlawing traditional and community-based healing practices. What emerged is a model that treated the body as a machine to be fixed, with industry supplying the parts (and profiting from a genius, if not evil, business model that creates and keeps lifelong customers).

If you're in the wellness world, you've been seeing this shift for the last few decades. Acute and trauma medicine remain indispensable (no herbal poultice can replace emergency surgery) but more and more people are recognizing the limits of a purely reactive model. A new paradigm is emerging that blends the strengths of Western biomedicine with holistic practices like nutrition, herbalism, breathwork, meditation, sound therapy, prayer, and energy healing. Preventative and integrative approaches are resurging, not as alternatives but as complements. People are relearning how to take care of themselves at home through tracking cycles, tending their nervous systems, and recognizing that health is not just physical but emotional, spiritual, and relational.

The shift ahead is not about rejecting modern medicine but about weaving it back into a broader concept of wellness where the body is not a broken machine to repair but a living instrument to tune. Success in health will be measured not just by lifespan, but by wholeness, coherence, and vitality.

School and Education

For much of the past century, schooling was designed less to cultivate human potential and more to produce reliable workers. The standardized curriculum of the 20th century mirrored the logic of the factory: bells marked shifts, desks were lined in rows, and memorization taking precedence over imagination. Schools doubled as glorified babysitting for the industrial economy, freeing parents for wage labor while training children to sit still, follow directions, and perform repetitive tasks. The result was one-size-fits-all education, usually defaulting to the lowest common denominator, with success measured in compliance rather than curiosity.

But this too was a historical detour. For most of human history, children learned the skills relevant for their life and future by *doing*. This looked like apprenticing with elders, absorbing seasonal and spiritual rhythms, contributing to household economies, and pursuing the crafts or trades of their communities. (I'm not glorifying this is any way—options were limited to say the least, and life was short. But the underlying concept is true.) In ancient Greece and Rome, education was reserved for elites but emphasized rhetoric, philosophy, and civic life. In medieval Europe, monasteries preserved knowledge while guilds trained young people in skills. Even in early America, before compulsory schooling, most learning happened at home, on farms, or through apprenticeships. The mass classroom model is relatively new and was explicitly designed to serve industrial society— a very distinct era in the human story that is coming to a close.

Now, parents and students alike are turning toward individualized learning. Homeschooling, microschools, and co-ops are proliferating. Alternative models like Montessori and Waldorf, which prioritize curiosity, embodiment, and imagination, are gaining traction. Online platforms and virtual communities have expanded access to knowledge, allowing children to follow their interests far beyond the walls of a single classroom. Increasingly, education is being designed not for conformity but for coherence: aligning with children's strengths, their nervous systems, and their natural curiosity.

This shift represents not the end of education but a return to the older concept of learning being contextual, embodied, and personalized. This also fits the future of work. It makes no sense to train and desensitize a child to a factor/industrial/corporate life that will not really exist by the time they are a working adult. The difference is that today's families can draw on both ancient wisdom and modern tools, blending apprenticeship-style learning with global access to knowledge. In the century ahead, success in education will not be measured by standardized tests but by resilience, creativity, and the capacity to keep learning across a lifetime.

Money and Economy

In the modern era wealth and power have flowed through centralized systems. National banks set monetary policy, corporations concentrated ownership, and ordinary people exchanged their labor for wages. This model, the hallmark of the 20th century, is rooted in centralized banking, wage dependence, and wealth reserved for the few.

In earlier ages, economies were far more diverse and decentralized. (Not necessarily better, but different.) Medieval Europe ran on local markets, guild economies, and bartering. Colonial America relied on a patchwork of local currencies, informal credit, and neighbor-to-neighbor lending. Even global empires managed trade through overlapping coinages and trust networks rather than uniform banking systems. For most of history, money was fluid, personal, and community-based instead of a monolithic structure imposed from above.

The industrial revolution, followed by the rise of modern nation-states, changed that. Central banking consolidated control: the Federal Reserve Act of 1913 gave the U.S. government and private banks enormous influence over the economy. The Bretton Woods system of 1944 tied global trade to the U.S. dollar, cementing an era of centralized monetary order. Then in 1971, President Nixon ended the dollar's direct convertibility to gold, ushering in the era of fiat currency and floating exchange rates. These systems created stability, but at the cost of diversity and resilience. By the mid-20th century, economic life for most people meant wage labor funneled into banks, mortgages, and corporations—a narrowing of possibility compared to older, more flexible arrangements.

Today, that centralized system is faltering. In its place, new forms of decentralization are beginning to surface. Cryptocurrencies and blockchain technology challenge the exclusive control of central banks. Local currencies, mutual aid networks, and community-based banking revive older traditions of trust-based exchange. Co-ops and peer-to-peer lending are quietly redistributing capital back to individuals rather than institutions. Digital platforms like Airbnb, Etsy, Patreon, and Substack allow people to earn directly from their creativity, land, or skills, bypassing traditional gatekeepers. Even the gig economy, with all its imperfections, signals a return to entrepreneurial survival, where resourcefulness and initiative begin to matter more than lifetime employment.

This is the same pattern repeating across sectors. Big agriculture is being challenged by homesteaders, regenerative farmers, and decentralized food networks. Big Pharma is being questioned by a growing movement toward herbalism, functional medicine, biohacking, frequency healing, and the like. Big media is losing ground to independent creators. Big education is being replaced by online mastery schools and peer-based learning communities. In every direction, the age of the centralized expert is giving way to a landscape of networks rather than hierarchies.

The future of money and economy will not be one grand system but many overlapping ones. Just as in the past, people will build wealth through diverse networks of exchange. Some digital, some local, some global, and some personal. What appears disruptive is actually a rediscovery that human economies thrive when they were plural, adaptive, and rooted in community.

Relationships and Family

For much of recorded history, marriage and family were less about love than survival. Marriage was an economic contract about land, lineage, labor, and alliance. In ancient Rome, marriage cemented political and economic ties. In medieval Europe, dowries and inheritance dictated unions and were often arranged without the couple's consent. Across most cultures, women's roles and value was tightly bound to reproduction, childrearing, and household labor, while men's roles were tied to provision and protection. Family was structured around duty, sacrifice, and rigid social norms.

The industrial era reshaped these roles but also reinforced their rigidity. Work moved out of the home and into factories, which created the nuclear family as an isolated unit of production and consumption. Basically, it became its own economic unit. Marriage became near-universal in the West by the mid-20th century, bound by legal codes and cultural expectations of lifelong commitment. Even as "romantic love" became the preferred justification, the structure of gendered duty remained. Divorce was stigmatized, childbearing was assumed, and the social order was built on conformity to these roles.

For many women today, partnerships are no longer compulsory for economic or social survival. Contraception, women's education and employment, and legal protections for divorce and same-sex marriage have opened space for choice. In the century ahead, marriage and family will likely continue to evolve into intentional partnerships formed around shared values rather than duty, co-living communities, and chosen families. Intergenerational households will re-emerge as housing and caregiving costs rise. Declining birth rates will reinforce this diversification, making small families—or networks of care that look more like tribes—the norm.

What will define the shift is consciousness.

Emotional intelligence, trauma awareness, and nervous system regulation are changing how parents relate to children and how partners relate to one another. Advances in psychology have introduced the language of attachment, boundaries, and relationship dynamics into mainstream parenting and marriage. Families are not only changing structure but also tone. They are becoming less about sacrifice and rigid roles, and more about integration, reciprocity, and care.

The family of the future will not look like the nuclear household idealized in the 1950s. It may look more like our deeper human past: fluid, adaptive, diverse, and communal, even tribal. But this time, it will carry the added dimension of choice.

Spirituality

I'll admit my bias up front. After spending years researching how goddess traditions were purposefully erased from religious memory, it is difficult for me to treat this topic as neutral. For most of recorded history, spiritual life was rooted in land, body, and cyclical belonging. The sacred was not administered from a throne or pulpit but embedded in seasonal rites, fertility cults, ancestor veneration, and temple-based economies led by priestesses.

That changed dramatically as power centralized. Particularly over the last two thousand years during the Piscean Age where religion shifted from local, embodied practices to hierarchical systems that defined the sacred from the top down. A distant, singular male creator deity replaced the many forms of the divine feminine and mother creator found in earlier cultures. Salvation narratives replaced initiation rites. Faith became something granted by an institution rather than cultivated through direct encounter.

In this model, truth was delivered from above, not revealed from within. Religion became perhaps even more so exoteric, meaning it focused on outer forms, correct doctrine, and obedience to appointed intermediaries. Mysticism, direct revelation, and feminine forms of knowing were either suppressed or reclassified as dangerous, heretical, or irrational. What was once cyclical and participatory became linear and male-administered: one god, one book, one truth, one acceptable path to salvation.

That balance is shifting. Institutional religion is declining in much of the industrialized world, while esoteric and mesoteric practices are rising into the mainstream. Yoga, astrology, meditation, plant medicine, and ancestral rituals are increasingly no longer fringe but woven into the daily lives of ordinary people. Spirituality and relationship to the divine is increasingly allowed to be personal rather than outsourced to authority. Historically, such surges of esotericism appear when exoteric structures lose credibility, like right now.

This does not mean that exoteric religion will disappear. Ritual, doctrine, and institutional belonging meet enduring human needs for stability and identity. What the Aquarian age brings is not replacement but decentralization. Authority disperses, the sacred pluralizes, and spirituality unfolds as a spectrum. Exoteric forms will continue, but they will increasingly share space with esoteric experiences (direct encounters with the divine) and mesoteric communities (allegorical interpretation, shared ritual, deeper symbolic teaching).

Within this larger spiritual shift, what many call Christ consciousness is moving out of the frame of a single historical figure and returning as a universal state of awareness. In early Christian mysticism, union with the divine was expressed as "the Father and I are one" and "the kingdom of heaven is within you." These were not metaphors for belief but descriptions of a direct interior experience available to all, not mediated by institution or clergy.

For two thousand years, Christ was cast primarily in a solar, masculine form: transcendent, disembodied, positioned above matter. Salvation was framed as escape, not integration. The body was treated as a problem to overcome, and the feminine was relegated to symbol rather than active principle. That is changing. The feminine dimension of the Christ impulse, known as Sophia, Shekhinah, Mary Magdalene, the Black Madonna, etc., has begun to resurface in culture and devotion. This is not a return to goddess worship in a nostalgic sense, but a rebalancing of the archetype: union over escape, embodiment over abstraction, cyclical wisdom over linear ascent.

To bring these two poles together is to recover the older mystical term *Anthropos*: the fully integrated human, both divine and embodied. In this light, gods and myths are not static figures but expressions of consciousness attempting to see and experience itself. They change as our perception changes, each age generating its own spiritual architecture. Pisces produced a savior and a distant, elusive heaven. Aquarius may produce archetypes of network, vibration, decentralization, and the return of immanent divinity through the feminine. I believe we are remembering that the divine was never outside us. It shifts form as consciousness evolves because it is consciousness reflecting itself back through matter.

Leadership and Power

For most of recorded history, leadership has been defined by strength, hierarchy, and control. From kings and emperors to generals and industrial tycoons, the strongman leader was the archetype of power: decisive, dominating, commanding loyalty through fear or charisma. Power was centralized, and survival often depended on obedience. This model is not surprising. Humans are wired for survival; our reptilian brains, instincts, and egos designed to seek security. Because of this, we are easily swayed by groupthink, blind to our biases, and susceptible to manipulation. We also love to form hierarchies as a way to find our place in the community. Even if we don't like where we fall in that hierarchy, our brain loves the sureness of it.

Power has often been associated with evil, because its pursuit has so frequently come from fear. Fear that there is *not enough* of resources, time, love, safety. Where scarcity dominates, so do power struggles. In this sense, much of human suffering has been tied to illusions of control and security. To cope, individuals and groups adopt roles within the power dynamic: sometimes oppressor, sometimes victim, but in the end whichever best secures a sense of safety. Power, in this light, has been a survival strategy as much as a political one.

But power itself is not inherently corrupt. It is a neutral force, shaped by how it is used. In the past three millennia, power has been predominantly expressed in masculine-coded forms: force, conquest, hierarchy, domination. To gain power was to take it, to push boundaries, to prove oneself through competition. This model fueled empires, nation-states, colonialism, and corporate capitalism. But it is also not "just the way things are" or inevitable, as we will find out.

The emerging paradigm suggests a shift toward feminine-coded forms of power. Rather than "power over," the future points toward "power with." Leadership is becoming more networked, distributed, and collective. Grassroots movements, co-ops, team-based projects, and smaller community-focused enterprises reflect this shift. Instead of demanding loyalty from the top down, leaders increasingly gain legitimacy by responding to what is needed and by unifying people around shared purpose.

This change resonates with insights from Human Design's "Cross of the Sleeping Phoenix," which includes the 34–20 channel of responsive power. This is a different kind of leadership: not the constant initiation of action, but the capacity to respond when the time is right. In this model, power is not grasped but received. It emerges situationally, when the leader's presence, clarity, and energy are called forth by circumstances. The task is not to push, but to manage energy, to wait, and to act decisively when the moment arrives.

History offers hints of this. Societies have not always been ruled solely by conquerors. Indigenous cultures often relied on councils, elders, or clan mothers whose authority was relational rather than coercive. Even within hierarchical empires, moments of responsive leadership appear—leaders who acted not by imposing their will but by discerning what their people needed at the right moment. Yet these were exceptions rather than norms. The coming cycle may bring this "yin" form of power to the forefront for the first time at scale.

It may feel hard to imagine, because written human history (which only goes back so far) has mostly known only yang. But feminine leadership— responsive, integrative, collective—offers the possibility of transforming power from domination into stewardship. In the next century, leadership may look less like the solitary strongman and more like networks of people, attuned and responsive, wielding power in service of coherence and survival together.

Tools of the Quantum Paradigm

This shift we are going through is not just mental or spiritual but also very physical.

If the last century gave us the machine, the factory, and the clock as its dominant tools, the next will give us subtler instruments: the nervous system, the subconscious, intuition, and embodied action. These are not luxuries but survival skills in a paradigm where consciousness, not matter, is the ground of reality.

To me, these are three "must dos" when it comes to weathering the transition into the new age:

1. Learn to Work with Emotional Energy

For generations, emotions were treated as inconveniences or weaknesses, and most definitely something to suppress, medicate, or hide. But modern psychology and trauma research have shown that our nervous systems are central to how we perceive and create reality. Regulation versus dysregulation shapes not only individual well-being but collective dynamics. Fight, flight, freeze, and fawn are not just personal responses—they ripple outward, affecting families, organizations, and nations.

In the coming paradigm, emotional awareness becomes baseline literacy. Parents teaching their children nervous system regulation is as foundational as teaching them to read or tie their shoes. Within a few generations, this could be standard knowledge. Just as public health campaigns in the 20th century taught handwashing, the 21st may teach somatic regulation, co-regulation, and the art of staying present under stress.

The subconscious is another layer of this emotional technology. Once dismissed or reduced to vague psychology, it is now understood as a primary driver of behavior. Belief patterns, trauma loops, and energetic imprints express themselves not just in individuals but in culture and institutions. Reprogramming the subconscious through somatic practice, hypnosis, pattern work, or symbolic systems like astrology and Human Design is already moving from fringe interest to practical skill. Historically, symbolic literacy was considered essential—there have only been two eras in Western history when astrology was actively dismissed: the "Dark Ages" and now. The shift ahead is from treating the mind as a machine to recognizing it as a field that can be tuned.

Embodiment is the final piece. The new paradigm doesn't separate spirituality from the body, or intellect from instinct. It asks us to live in our bodies as instruments capable of sensing, responding, and transmitting coherence. The body is no longer the machine to be managed but the antenna through which consciousness speaks.

2. Take Aligned Action

If awareness and regulation are the foundation, action is the expression. One danger of living in an age of transition is becoming trapped in reflection, endlessly analyzing the liminal space. Or write an entire book about it (geez).

But the new paradigm requires participation. And all the yang/air/fire energy over the next decade or so will help with that! Ideas arrive like seeds through the collective unconscious, or an "idea distribution system," as mischievous and precise as the cat distribution system. They land on you because they resonate with your frequency.

The choice is simple: say yes and incarnate them, or say no and watch them move on to someone else. Writing the book, buying the land, birthing the children, planting the garden, starting the business—these are not just personal choices but acts of stewardship. They are how new worlds are built.

This is where the integration of feminine and masculine dynamics *within* becomes crucial. The feminine feels, trusts, and receives the seed, or idea. The masculine shapes, builds, and manifests it. Together, they create coherence. Too much surrender without action, and the seed rots. Too much action without alignment, and the effort burns out. The task is to find resonance and then move decisively when the call comes.

3. Live in Rhythm with Cycles

Linear time is breaking down, and with it the illusion of endless growth. What replaces it is cyclical and spiral time. Just as ancient societies lived by the rhythms of seasons, moons, and stars, the coming paradigm will re-anchor life in patterns of renewal.

This doesn't mean returning to superstition; it means reintegrating what modern science now validates—circadian biology, lunar and hormonal rhythms, seasonal cycles, and the larger astronomical patterns traced throughout this book. Astrology, at its root, is the study of rhythm and resonance. It reminds us that energy moves in waves, not lines, and that our bodies and emotions are attuned to those cosmic tides whether we realize it or not.

Living in rhythm means learning how to honor these energetic ebbs and flows. This may look like working with transits, moon phases, and personal cycles as allies rather than obstacles. It may means aligning rest, creativity, and community with natural timing instead of forcing life into mechanical schedules. Resilience grows when we embrace the pulse of life itself—birth, death, integration, renewal—and let those movements guide the shape of our days.

4. Build Communities of Coherence

Humans have always survived in tribes, but the industrial age fractured us into nuclear families and isolated individuals. The next hundred years may see a return to more tribal patterns like intergenerational households and intentional communities.

The difference this time is awareness. Communities will not just be about survival but about coherence: groups that regulate together, create together, and embody shared values. Whether through co-ops, microschools, or shared land projects, small communities will function as the crucibles of resilience and innovation.

5. Reclaim Story and Myth/Spirituality

Every paradigm shift comes with new stories. Myths of the old age, like conquest, sacrifice, and martyr/victim archetypes, are unraveling. (I might be bullish on this one, but it is my hope). In their place, new archetypes and metaphors are being born. The goddess is returning, not as a symbol of domination but of death/rebirth and reciprocity. The spiral is replacing the line as the image of time. Networks and webs are replacing thrones and ladders as the image of power.

Story is not just a nice thing to pass the time. It is a powerful code that programs consciousness. To tell new stories is to seed new realities. In the quantum paradigm, reclaiming myth and weaving new narrative threads is one of the most powerful tools we have. Together, these principles and tools form the operating system of the quantum paradigm. They are how we bridge theory into practice, ideas into embodiment, collapse into coherence. They are how we midwife the new world.

The Only Constant is Change

This all feels so sticky because most industrialized societies are addicted to change but afraid of transformation. We chase the dopamine rush of newness through new technologies, trends, and ideas, while resisting the deeper shifts that ask us to surrender control. Change is something we can plan, measure, and manage. Transformation is not.

Transformation moves slowly. It's the long steady march of becoming that sweeps through our lives, often against our will. You can see it coming, you can even resist it for a time, but you can't stop it. It is the force that brings every cycle to completion and renewal.

The paradox at the heart of transformation is that it requires both awareness and surrender. You can't force it, and you can't avoid it. The only choice you have is how consciously you meet it. The more we cling to the familiar, the more painful the process becomes. The moment we loosen our grip, we begin to see that the disintegration of the old is not preparation, not punishment.

Fear naturally arises in these moments. The key here is that fear does not mean something is wrong, but that something new is being born. Fear shows us where our current beliefs and frameworks no longer fit reality. When we learn to meet it with presence instead of panic, fear transforms into courage. It becomes the energy that fuels creation rather than the resistance that blocks it.

Ancient systems like the *I Ching*, *Tarot*, and astrology all describe this process in their own languages. The *I Ching's* "Turning Point" hexagram teaches that transformation unfolds through nature's own timing, not force. The *Death* and *Tower* cards in the Tarot remind us that endings are necessary precursors to renewal. In astrology, Scorpio and the eighth house govern the mysteries of death, rebirth, and alchemy, or the transmutation of one state into another.

Across cultures, the snake has long symbolized this process. It sheds its skin again and again, renewing itself without losing its essence. The serpent coiled around the world tree, the Ouroboros swallowing its own tail (featured on the cover), and Quetzalcoatl the feathered serpent all speak to the same truth: creation and destruction are not opposites but partners in the same dance. The witch's cauldron represents archetype of the great cosmic womb where the old is dissolved so that the new can take form.

And man, do all of these symbols nail the current moment. Many of the structures that once seemed unsinkable are taking on water. It's uncomfortable, but necessary. Remember, transformation never asks for permission, it simply offers participation.

In a world overwhelmed by constant noise, sovereignty becomes the essential spiritual act. To be sovereign is not to isolate or control, but to return to one's own center. To your body, intuition, and inner knowing. Our energy follows our attention, and attention is the purest form of power we have. What we focus on, grows. When our attention is hijacked by media, fear, or outrage we surrender that power. When we consciously choose what to give our energy to, we begin to reshape our reality.

This is the real awakening of our time. Not to a single belief or ideology, but to the responsibility of consciousness itself. The courage to know what ours is to hold, *and what is not*. The willingness to release what no longer fits, even without knowing what comes next. Transformation is never easy, but it is always honest. It strips away illusion until only truth remains. And when we meet it willingly, we find that death is not the end of the story. It's simply the moment the light returns.

This process is now unfolding in multiple layers from generation to civilization. What we are experiencing isn't just political upheaval or technological change but a collective *initiation*. We are being invited to evolve from control to coherence, from domination to participation, from separation to relationship. The question is not whether transformation will happen, but how consciously we will move through it.

Your Sacred Assignment

At its root, *apocalypse* never meant destruction but unveiling. To pass through an apocalypse is not to endure the end of the world, but to cross a threshold where illusions are stripped away and new realities come into view. It is initiation, descent, and portal.

The old civic order is falling away. Institutions built on hierarchy, endless growth, and mechanistic control are straining under their contradictions. Our sacred assignment, individually and collectively, is not to duct-tape them back together, but to release them with reverence and turn our energy toward the new. Cycles are ending—beliefs, structures, ways of organizing society. The invitation is not clinging out of fear, but conscious creation out of hope.

Apocalypse was the descent. The Quantum Paradigm is the ascent. We are still walking through the underworld which means it is, and will continue to be, messy, nonlinear, and ambiguous. And as we being to emerge on the other side we will realize that we are not met with utopia, but a new set of challenges.

So what do we do now?

First, we stop feeding the spiral of fear. We learn to steady ourselves from the inside out through nervous system regulation, awareness of our own energy, and a return to inner authority. This is not about bypassing reality. It is about meeting it with coherence. We can no longer outsource our discernment to experts, priests, psychics, institutions, or governments. Guidance has its place, but not as a substitute for our own knowing. The task is to rebuild trust in our bodies, our intuition, and our direct relationship with what is real. Sovereignty and relationship are not opposites. Like healthy ecosystems, true interdependence begins with strong, rooted individuals.

The work of this time is simple, but not easy.

Stay coherent. Remember who we are. Protect what is sacred. Plant what wants to grow.

Remember that change is not a disruption to the norm. **It is the norm**.

Build, not as a reaction, but as an act of devotion to what is trying to be born through us. We are not here just to survive the ending of an old world. We are here to participate in the beginning of the next one.

And with that we return to where we began: cycles as the structure of reality, collapse as initiation, and consciousness as the real field of history. The rest will be written by how we choose to meet this moment.

* * *

You have been telling people that this is the Eleventh Hour, now you must go back and tell the people that this is the Hour.

And there are things to be considered...

Where are you living?
What are you doing?
What are your relationships?
Are you in right relation?

Where is your water?

Know your garden.
It is time to speak your truth.
Create your community.
Be good to each other.
And do not look outside yourself for your leader.

Then he clasped his hands together, smiled, and said:
This could be a good time!
There is a river flowing now very fast.
It is so great and swift that there are those who will be afraid.
They will try to hold on to the shore.
They will feel they are being torn apart and will suffer greatly.
Know the river has its destination.
The elders say we must let go of the shore,
push off into the middle of the river, keep our eyes open, and our heads above the
water.
And I say, see who is in there with you and celebrate.

At this time in history, we are to take nothing personally, least of all ourselves.
For the moment that we do, our spiritual growth and journey come to a halt.
The time of the lone wolf is over.

Gather yourselves!
Banish the word 'struggle' from your attitude and your vocabulary.
All that we do now must be done in a sacred manner and in celebration.

We are the ones we've been waiting for.

—Hopi Elders' Prophecy, June 8, 2000

Appendix A

Age of Libra (15,100–12,950 BCE)

The Age of Libra marked a transitional period where early humans began to balance survival with the first signs of cultural development. During this time, human groups expanded into new regions, including the significant migration across the Bering Land Bridge from Siberia into the Americas. This movement required cooperation, shared resource management, and adaptive social structures, aligning with Libra's themes of relationship and mutual support.

Evidence from this era shows an increase in trade networks and exchange of goods like obsidian, pigments, and shells across long distances. These exchanges suggest the early formation of intergroup agreements and systems of reciprocity. Survival was still central, but it was becoming tied to social coordination rather than pure individual endurance.

This period also gave rise to some of the earliest known examples of symbolic culture. The Lascaux Cave Paintings in present-day France, dating to approximately 15,000–13,000 BCE, show a clear shift in consciousness. These images of animals and hunting scenes were placed in deep, intentional spaces rather than public areas, indicating the emergence of ritual, artistic intention, and early symbolic language. The act of recording experience visually marks a turning point in cognitive development and reflects a growing capacity for abstraction and shared meaning.

The Age of Libra ended abruptly around 12,950 BCE with the onset of the Younger Dryas, a sudden return to glacial conditions. Some researchers associate this shift with a comet impact or similar cosmic event. The resulting extinction of large Ice Age animals forced rapid human adaptation and set the conditions for the next phase of development. With the Age of Virgo, humanity began moving slowly toward early agriculture and settled life. Although the Age of Libra closed in hardship, it established three foundations that would shape later civilization: large-scale migration, emerging trade networks, and the first clear evidence of aesthetic and symbolic culture.

Age of Virgo (12,950–10,800 BCE)

The Age of Virgo marked a shift from pure nomadism toward intentional interaction with the land. Virgo is associated with harvest, precision, and practical organization, and this period reflects those qualities in the emerging foundations of agriculture and early settlement patterns. In regions such as the Levant and along the Nile, groups began harvesting wild grains using specialized tools like sickle blades and grinding stones. These practices represent the earliest known steps toward food cultivation and stored surplus, which would later enable permanent settlement.

Cultures such as the Isnan along the Nile developed in a climate that was wetter and more fertile than today, taking advantage of abundant resources. This period also saw major environmental disruptions, including significant flooding around 10,500 BCE, which caused sudden abandonment of some sites. If an advanced coastal or riverine culture existed before widespread cataclysmic events, this era would align with its rise, reflecting Virgo's association with craft, skill, and mastery of material processes.

The Natufian culture in the Levant, active from around 12,000 to 9,000 BCE, is one of the clearest examples of this shift. The Natufians cultivated cereals, produced some of the earliest known bread around 12,000 BCE, and brewed fermented beverages by approximately 11,000 BCE. These developments show a clear move toward transformation and refinement of raw resources, consistent with Virgo's themes. They also established semi-permanent settlements, leading toward later urban centers such as Jericho in the following Age of Leo.

Animal domestication also began during this time. Evidence suggests pigs were tamed around 13,000–12,700 BCE, sheep between 11,000 and 9,000 BCE, and the earliest fully domesticated dog appears in a burial dated to around 12,200 BCE. These findings show that humans were beginning to form ongoing, managed relationships with animals, indicating developing roles of caretaking and service within early communities.

As the last Ice Age ended, climates stabilized, and humans responded by refining survival strategies. Pottery appears in this period in its earliest forms, and hunter-gatherer cultures became more specialized and regionally distinct. Full agriculture had not yet taken hold, but the groundwork for it had been established. Communities began tracking seasonal cycles more precisely, hinting at emerging calendrical systems and organized observation of natural rhythms. The Age of Virgo represents the beginning of deliberate human planning and environmental management, laying the structural base for the agricultural societies that would soon arise.

Age of Leo (10,800–8,650 BCE)

The Age of Leo corresponds with the final retreat of the Ice Age and the beginning of more stable climates that allowed complex human activity to take root. Although Leo is associated with solar energy and creative emergence, the early part of this period was marked by severe disruption. The Younger Dryas cold event, beginning around 10,900 BCE, brought a rapid return to glacial conditions that halted agricultural experimentation and forced human groups to adapt quickly. Around 9,600 BCE, a sudden warming event triggered large-scale flooding and rising sea levels, contributing to the disappearance of coastal settlements and possibly inspiring later flood myths found across global traditions. Volcanic activity in regions such as the Virunga Mountains also altered river systems like the Nile, reshaping the geography of early human settlement.

As conditions stabilized, humans began forming the first recognizable foundations of civilization. Evidence from Mesopotamia shows the domestication of sheep, goats, cattle, and pigs between roughly 11,000 and 9,000 BCE, alongside the cultivation of early grains such as wheat and barley. In the Levant, the settlement at Jericho transitioned from a Natufian campsite to a permanent town by around 9,600 BCE, signaling an early shift toward urban development. In North America, cultural traditions began to take shape through distinctive basketry and early pottery among emerging tribal groups.

One of the most significant archaeological discoveries linked to this era is Göbekli Tepe in modern-day Turkey. Built around 9,600 BCE by hunter-gatherer groups, it is considered the oldest known ceremonial complex. The site features megalithic pillars carved with animals and symbolic imagery and shows deliberate astronomical alignment, including orientation toward the Cygnus constellation. These features indicate an early form of organized ritual culture and an awareness of celestial patterns that predates settled agricultural life.

The Age of Leo is also associated with the lion symbolism found in later monumental architecture. The Great Sphinx of Giza is commonly dated to around 2500 BCE, but some geological studies have proposed a far earlier origin based on erosion patterns consistent with heavy rainfall. If this interpretation is correct, structures like the Sphinx and other megalithic sites, including the Osireion in Egypt or submerged ruins such as Yonaguni and Dwarka, may reflect remnants of pre-cataclysmic cultures from this era.

The Age of Leo marks a turning point in human development. It reflects the transition from survival under extreme climatic pressure to the first stable experiments in settlement, ritual architecture, and organized food production. It is in this window that the earliest hints of what would later become civilization begin to appear.

Age of Cancer (8,650–6,500 BCE)

The Age of Cancer corresponds with the consolidation of agricultural life and the rise of settled village cultures. Cancer is associated with nurturing, home, and the protective principle, and during this period human communities began establishing stable settlements focused on food security, fertility, and continuity. Domestication that began in earlier ages became established practice. By around 8,500 BCE, cattle, pigs, goats, and sheep were managed across regions spanning Anatolia, Mesopotamia, the Indus region, and southeastern Europe. Barley and wheat cultivation expanded between 8,000 and 7,000 BCE, and early grain processing produced beer-like brews, porridges, and later bread.

Permanent settlements developed around reliable water sources, particularly along the Nile and in northern Mesopotamia. The presence of food surplus led to increased population density and new forms of communal organization. Pottery emerged around this time, especially in Mesopotamia and Anatolia, often decorated with fertility imagery, including depictions of pregnant figures that suggest reverence for a mother deity. These motifs reflect the growing cultural emphasis on nourishment and protection, central themes of the Cancer archetype.

Evidence of early fortifications appears in this era as well. Jericho, already developing in the Age of Leo, constructed substantial defensive walls and a stone tower around 8,000 BCE. These structures suggest organized labor and an emerging concern with safeguarding life and resources, whether from flooding or human threats. In Anatolia, sites such as Nevali Cori and Çayönü followed Göbekli Tepe, which was deliberately buried around 8,000 BCE. These newer settlements maintained ritual spaces with stone pillars, indicating continuity of symbolic and ceremonial practices.

Çatalhöyük, active from approximately 7,500 to 5,500 BCE, represents one of the earliest examples of proto-urban life. Its inhabitants practiced mixed subsistence, combining farming with hunting. Ritual bull iconography and shrines dedicated to a female fertility figure suggest a culture centered on household ritual and seasonal renewal. The significance of cattle and bovine symbolism appears here centuries before the Age of Taurus, indicating that astrological animal archetypes may stem from much older symbolic associations.

Outside of the Near East, permanent dwellings also began to appear. In Britain, a Mesolithic timber structure in Northumberland dated to around 7,800 BCE shows early settlement activity. The site of Stonehenge was already known as a ritual landscape by this period, with evidence of a wooden ceremonial structure in use as early as 8,600 BCE.

By the end of this era, many of the Ice Age megafauna, including woolly rhinoceros, giant elk, and cave predators, had gone extinct, marking a definitive ecological transition. Genetic research identifies the period from roughly 8,000 to 3,000 BCE as the Identical Ancestor Point, meaning that all living humans today likely descend from a population that existed during this timeframe. In symbolic terms, this aligns with the Age of Cancer's association with ancestry and origins. Copper use and fermentation practices also began to appear, signaling growing experimental engagement with materials and transformation processes that would define later ages.

Age of Gemini (6,500–4,350 BCE)

The Age of Gemini marks a shift toward communication, exchange, and increasing cultural complexity. Gemini is associated with connection and the movement of ideas, and during this period the foundations of trade networks, proto-writing, and early urban development began to take shape. Twin symbolism, often linked to Gemini, appears in figurines and dual-figure motifs found in Neolithic settlements like Çatalhöyük, showing that the archetype was active long before formal astrology was codified.

This era saw the emergence of symbolic communication systems that served practical functions rather than purely ritual ones. Proto-writing developed independently in several regions, including the Vinca culture of Southeast Europe, early Chinese settlements, and West Asia. Clay tokens and marked pottery were used to track goods and agricultural surplus, and these systems gradually evolved into inscribed tablets. While full writing systems would not appear until the next age, the foundations of record-keeping, accounting, and symbolic notation begin here.

Early civilization-building processes also accelerated. In Mesopotamia, the Ubaid period (6,500–3,800 BCE) introduced large-scale irrigation, social stratification, and organized ceremonial centers. These developments laid the groundwork for the city-states of Sumer. In Egypt, Neolithic farming communities along the Nile consolidated and began developing stable settlement patterns and regional identities. In the Indus region, pre-Harappan cultures emerged around 5,500 BCE, setting the stage for one of the world's earliest planned urban systems. In Europe, the Vinca culture (5,700–4,500 BCE) produced distinctive ceramics and symbolic markings that some researchers believe may represent an early script. The islands of Malta saw their first farming populations arrive between 5,200 and 4,000 BCE, initiating a cultural lineage that would later produce megalithic temple complexes.

Climatic shifts played a role in accelerating these developments. Around 6,000 BCE, global temperatures declined after a warm period, contributing to the final retreat of the Laurentide Ice Sheet in North America. As regions like Mesopotamia and East Africa became more arid, populations adapted by settling near dependable water sources and organizing labor for irrigation and food storage. These pressures encouraged social communication, planning, and trade between emerging settlements.

The Age of Gemini represents the early formation of networks, symbols, goods, and ideas. It marks the beginning of intentional communication beyond immediate kin groups and a move toward systems that connected people across distance. These foundations would expand rapidly in the following Age of Taurus with the rise of monumental architecture, full writing systems, and established state religions.

Age of Taurus (4,350–2,200 BCE)

The Age of Taurus corresponds with the expansion of agriculture, the rise of stable civilizations, and the widespread veneration of the bull as a symbol of fertility, strength, and continuity. Taurus was regarded as the first zodiac sign in Mesopotamian star lore because it rose with the spring equinox during this era. Agricultural life became central, and many cultures expressed this shift through fertility cults, bull symbolism, and rituals tied to seasonal cycles.

In Mesopotamia, the Uruk period (4,000–3,100 BCE) brought early urban development, organized labor, and the emergence of proto-cuneiform writing used for tracking grain, land, and trade. This evolved into fully developed writing systems by around 2,600 BCE, marking the beginning of recorded history. City-states like Uruk and Ur became religious and administrative centers, with temples dedicated to grain deities and seasonal renewal.

In Egypt, Neolithic farming communities along the Nile consolidated into the Old Kingdom (c. 3,150–2,181 BCE). Deities such as Hathor, associated with motherhood and nourishment, and the Apis bull, symbolizing life-force and royal authority, became central figures in religious practice. Monumental architecture, including the construction of the Great Pyramid around 2,560 BCE, reflects the era's emphasis on permanence, structure, and agricultural stability.

The sacred bull motif also appears prominently in the Minoan civilization on Crete (c. 3,700–1,450 BCE). Bull-leaping scenes at Knossos and the recurring labrys symbol reflect ritual activity centered on strength, fertility, and cyclical renewal. In the Indus Valley, the mature Harappan phase (2,600–1,900 BCE) developed distinct urban planning, standardized weights, trade networks, and iconography that often featured bulls and cattle. These cultures showed increasing central organization and reliance on agricultural surplus as the basis for economic and social systems.

Megalithic structures in Europe, such as Newgrange in Ireland (c. 3,200 BCE) and Stonehenge in Britain (c. 3,000–2,000 BCE), indicate a deepening interest in astronomical alignment and seasonal timing. These sites reflect a growing connection between agriculture, ritual, and the observation of celestial cycles, consistent with Taurus's association with earth-based stability and repetition.

Environmental change also shaped this era. Around 3,500 BCE, North Africa underwent rapid desertification, transforming the Sahara and pushing populations toward river valleys, particularly the Nile. In Mesopotamia, shifting rainfall patterns and river courses contributed to increased organization around irrigation and flood management. These pressures encouraged complex administrative systems and reinforced religious narratives centered on survival, fertility, and seasonal rebirth.

By the end of the Age of Taurus, the first territorial empires began to emerge. The Akkadian Empire under Sargon (2,334–2,218 BCE) unified the Sumerian city-states, marking a transition from local sacred kingship to centralized imperial rule. In Egypt, the collapse of the Old Kingdom around 2,181 BCE led to the First Intermediate Period, a time of decentralization that set the stage for political restructuring in the next age. The symbols and systems that arose during the Age of Taurus—agriculture, organized worship, monumental architecture, and the sacred bull—remained influential long after the constellation shifted from the equinox, continuing to shape religious and cultural forms well into the Bronze Age.

Age of Aries (2,200 BCE–50 BCE)

The Age of Aries marked a shift from agrarian fertility cultures toward martial societies defined by conquest, hierarchy, and personal heroism. Aries is associated with iron, warfare, ambition, and pioneering force, and this period reflects those qualities through the rise of warrior-kings, standing armies, and territorial empires. Civilizations began organizing around military power rather than purely agricultural surplus, and social prestige became linked to conquest, law, and individual authority.

In Mesopotamia, the Akkadian Empire unified the Sumerian city-states and introduced the model of imperial domination that would be repeated throughout this era. Successive powers such as the Babylonians and Assyrians expanded through organized warfare, developing legal codes, astronomy, and literature. The Epic of Gilgamesh, composed between 2100 and 1200 BCE, stands as one of the earliest recorded hero narratives, emphasizing personal glory and the quest for legacy, both hallmarks of Arian consciousness.

The Hittites, emerging around 1600 BCE in Anatolia, mastered ironworking and initiated the Iron Age. The spread of iron weaponry gave rise to new forms of military expansion across Eurasia. In the Aegean, the Mycenaean civilization thrived, culminating in the conflict memorialized as the Trojan War around 1250 BCE. Its fall and the later arrival of the Dorians reshaped Greek society and set the foundations for the Classical Greek world.

In Egypt, the ram-headed deity Amun rose to prominence during the instability following the Old Kingdom. Amun merged with the solar god Ra to become Amun-Ra, a symbol of royal power and divine authority. Pharaohs adopted ram imagery, reinforcing the connection between rulership and martial divinity. Similar themes appear in other cultures as the sacred bull of the previous age gradually gave way to the ram as a symbol of decisive action, sacrifice, and personal agency.

Religious narratives during this era reflect this symbolic shift. In the Hebrew tradition, the story of Abraham sacrificing a ram in place of his son marks a clear replacement of bull symbolism with ram imagery. Later, Moses denounces the Golden Calf, further signaling the rejection of the previous Age of Taurus. In Persia, the Mithraic tradition features the slaying of the bull, although the surviving Roman imagery appears closer to the transition into Pisces and may represent a reinterpretation of older ritual symbolism.

This era also includes the Axial Age (800–300 BCE), a period of major intellectual and spiritual development. Figures such as Confucius, Lao Tzu, Buddha, Pythagoras, Socrates, and Plato laid down the philosophical and ethical frameworks that continue to shape global thought. These teachings emerged at a time when societies were grappling with the consequences of militarized expansion and seeking new principles to guide human conduct.

The final centuries of the Age of Aries saw the rise of Rome, founded in 753 BCE. Rome embodied Arian themes through its focus on discipline, military infrastructure, and codified law. Greek city-states also reached their cultural peak during this period, advancing philosophy, democracy, and science—fields driven by inquiry and individual agency.

The Age of Aries was characterized by conflict, empire-building, and intellectual breakthroughs born from social strain. As the Age of Pisces approached, the emphasis on external conquest began to give way to themes of inner devotion, sacrifice, and spiritual redemption, preparing the ground for the next major shift in human consciousness.

Age of Pisces (50 BCE–2100 CE)

The Age of Pisces corresponds with the rise of faith-based systems, global religions, and large hierarchical institutions built around belief and devotion. Pisces is associated with spirituality, surrender, sacrifice, and illusion. These themes are reflected in the development of monotheistic religions, imperial expansion under religious banners, and the emergence of universal ideologies that attempted to unite humanity under shared doctrines.

This age began around the time the Roman Republic collapsed and the Roman Empire rose to dominance. The Pax Romana created the infrastructure for new belief systems to spread. Christianity emerged within this context. Its early symbols, including the fish and references to fishermen, align with Piscean imagery. Jesus's teachings on compassion, sacrifice, and universal love became defining themes of the era. When Emperor Constantine adopted Christianity in the 4th century CE, spiritual authority fused with political power, setting the model for centralized religious institutions throughout the age.

Islam appeared in the 7th century CE and followed a similar pattern of rapid expansion, religious consolidation, and administrative unity. The Islamic Caliphates became centers of scholarship, trade, and spiritual life, contributing to the preservation and transmission of ancient knowledge.

Sufi traditions emphasized direct spiritual experience, reflecting the mystical dimension of Pisces. Buddhism, expanding from India into East and Southeast Asia, also developed strong institutional structures while carrying forward themes of compassion, detachment, and transcendence.

Throughout the Middle Ages, the Catholic Church held significant influence over European political structures, law, and daily life. Religious institutions provided continuity but also enforced control, highlighting the Piscean duality between genuine spiritual search and rigid doctrine. Faith was both a unifying force and a tool of authority.

Pisces is also linked to illusion and ideological conflict. The Age of Exploration spread Christianity globally, often under the banner of salvation while enforcing colonization and cultural erasure. The Scientific Revolution challenged religious dominance and introduced a new form of universal belief rooted in rationality and empirical knowledge. The Enlightenment extended this trend by emphasizing individual rights and secular governance. Yet even these new systems carried Piscean traits, offering overarching visions meant to bind society into shared ideals.

The 20th century intensified these dynamics. Global wars were fought not only over territory but over competing belief systems, whether religious or ideological. Concepts like martyrdom, sacrifice for the nation, and ideological purity reflect Piscean extremes. In response, institutions such as the United Nations emerged, promoting global cooperation and collective security.

As the Age of Pisces nears its end, its structures are beginning to dissolve. Organized religion is declining in influence, trust in large institutions is eroding, and globalist narratives are losing coherence. The themes of sacrifice and external salvation are giving way to an emphasis on autonomy, networked systems, and direct engagement—an early signal of the coming Aquarian age. The Age of Pisces established the framework for global consciousness through religion, empire, and ideology. The next age will challenge those forms and ask humanity to participate in connection with more agency and clarity.

Sources, Influences & Further Study

Cycle Research & Long-Wave Theories

- Cycles Research Institute Archives (https://cyclesresearchinstitute.org)
- Raymond H. Wheeler — *War, 599 B.C.–1950 A.D.*
- Edward R. Dewey — *Cycles: The Science of Prediction*
- Foundation for the Study of Cycles
- Nikolai Kondratiev — *The Long Waves in Economic Life*
- William Strauss & Neil Howe — *The Fourth Turning*
- Immanuel Wallerstein — *The Modern World-System* and *World-Systems Analysis: An Introduction*
- Paul Kennedy — *The Rise and Fall of the Great Powers*
- George Friedman — *The Next 100 Years* and *The Storm Before the Calm*
- Peter Zeihan — *The End of the World Is Just the Beginning*
- James Dale Davidson & Lord William Rees-Mogg — *The Sovereign Individual*
- Ray Dalio — *Principles for Dealing with the Changing World Order*

Astrological, Archetypal & Planetary Cycles

- Richard Tarnas — *Cosmos and Psyche* and *The Passion of the Western Mind*
- Dane Rudhyar — *The Planetarization of Consciousness*
- André Barbault — *Planetary Cycles: Mundane Astrology*
- H.S. Green, Raphael & C.E.O. Carter — *Mundane Astrology*
- Christine Skinner — *Exploring Financial Astrology*
- Benson Bobrick — *The Fated Sky*

- Jessica Davidson — Astrological essays on Uranus, Neptune, and Pluto cycles (jessicadavidson.co.uk)
- Ra Uru Hu — *Human Design: The Science of Differentiation*

Mythic Time, Sacred Cosmology & Ancient Sky Traditions

- Giorgio de Santillana & Hertha von Dechend — *Hamlet's Mill*
- *The Enuma Elish* — Babylonian Creation Epic (1100–1200 BCE)
- *Dead Sea Scrolls / Book of Enoch* — Astronomical Book and Solar Covenant Calendar
- Vedic Texts — *Rig Veda, Vedanga Jyotisha, Surya Siddhanta*
- Sri Yukteswar — *The Holy Science* (Yuga reinterpretation)
- Hopi Four Worlds Prophecy (Indigenous oral cosmology)
- David Graeber & David Wengrow — *The Dawn of Everything*
- Chris Gosden — *Magic: A History*
- C.G. Jung — *The Undiscovered Self*

A Note to the Reader

This book is a bridge between many disciplines. I spent over five years researching, thinking about, writing, re-writing, and re-writing some more. Over those years, my work drew from academic research, systems theory, astrology, mythic frameworks, lectures, and ongoing conversations with thinkers across disciplines. Some influences are cited directly, while others became part of the background of my thinking and may not be individually named.

My goal was to integrate historical cycles, structural analysis, and consciousness studies into one clear framework for understanding how societies break down and rebuild. This list of sources reflects the range of material that informed that work.

About the Author

Marissa Kester is a professional historian and astrologer with a background in military intelligence analysis. She specializes in tracking long-range social, economic, and spiritual cycles to identify emerging civilizational patterns. With fifteen years of analytical experience in cultural and geopolitical history, she brings a sharp, interdisciplinary lens to pattern recognition. Integrating archival research, strategic forecasting, and planetary intelligence, she maps the deeper structures of change that influence nations, bodies, and belief systems.

Equal parts historian, writer, and intuitive guide, Marissa translates complex civilizational patterns into language that makes sense for people who are trying to raise children, build a resilient life, and still make it to soccer practice while the world comes undone. Her work blends academic rigor with feminine intuition and a dry sense of humor, offering clarity without retreating into either cynicism or escapism.

She lives along the 30A stretch of the Florida Gulf Coast with her husband, three children, and a growing archive of books, herbal tinctures, and dogs.

She shares her ongoing work on Substack and YouTube, where she teaches history, astrology, sovereignty, and cyclical living for a new era.

You can connect with me on:
- https://www.youtube.com/@marissasacredthreads
- https://rebellehistory.substack.com

Also by Marissa Kester

There From the Beginning: Women in the US Air Force (Air University Press, 2021)
Women have been part of the U.S. Air Force since day one. Long before they were officially recognized, they were shaping history in ways that often went unseen. *There From the Beginning* dives into the untold stories of the women who helped build, serve, and lead in the Air Force, from its earliest days to the present.

This book is a deep, meticulously researched look at the evolving roles, challenges, and triumphs of women in the Air Force. It's not just about policies and progress; it's about the real women who defied expectations, pushed boundaries, and redefined what was possible.

Whether you're a history buff, a military professional, or just someone who loves stories of resilience and trailblazing women, *There From the Beginning* offers an insightful, engaging look at a history that deserves to be remembered.

Cycle Magic

Your cycle isn't just something to "deal with"—it's a built-in roadmap to energy, creativity, and deeper self-awareness. *Cycle Magic* is about shifting the way you see your menstrual cycle, from something to suppress or control to something that actually works *for* you.

Blending history, science, and ancient wisdom, this book unpacks the natural intelligence of your cycle and how to align your life with its rhythms. You'll learn how each phase influences your energy, emotions, and intuition and how to work *with* those shifts instead of fighting against them. Whether you want to optimize your productivity, deepen your connection to your body, or bring more ease into your daily life, *Cycle Magic* is your guide.

This is for anyone who's ever wondered: *What if my body actually knows what it's doing?*

www.ingramcontent.com/pod-product-compliance
Lightning Source LLC
Chambersburg PA
CBHW031019160726
47991CB00005B/1780